THE ISAIAH ENCOUNTER

"Chris Atkins is one of those rare individuals that God has clearly called to equip the church to worship. As an accomplished speaker, songwriter, and musician, he calls the church to move beyond music to engage in real worship and leads people beyond excellence to authenticity. Chris has a deep understanding of worship from the Word and practices amazing sensitivity to the Spirit's leading as he leads others into the presence of God. Above all, Chris is the most prolific equipper of worship leaders that I have ever known."

—**Ivan Veldhuizen**, Executive Director of International Ministries, Converge Worldwide

"Chris's unique gifting, seasoned experience, and biblical conviction make him a tremendous resource for the church in the area of worship. He has a keen understanding of why a life of worship needs to be the foundation for the corporate gathering time (Rom. 12:1). Chris has a great way of coupling timeless biblical worship principles with current cultural practices and training others to do likewise. He models what it means to make disciples who can make disciples in the vital area of worship ministry."

—**Dr. J. Michael Sager**, Senior Pastor, Faith Church, Austin, MN

THE ISAIAH ENCOUNTER

Living an Everyday Life of
WORSHIP

c h r i s   a t k i n s

New York

THE ISAIAH ENCOUNTER

Living an Everyday Life of Worship

Published in New York, New York, by Morgan James Publishing. Morgan James and The Entrepreneurial Publisher are trademarks of Morgan James, LLC.
www.MorganJamesPublishing.com

The Morgan James Speakers Group can bring authors to your live event. For more information or to book an event visit The Morgan James Speakers Group at
www.TheMorganJamesSpeakersGroup.com.

Unless otherwise indicated, scripture comes from the Holy Bible, New International Version˚, NIV˚ Copyright ©1973, 1978, 1984, 2011 by Biblica, Inc.˚ Used by permission. All rights reserved worldwide.

Scripture marked NASB comes from the New American Standard Bible, Copyright © 1960, 1962, 1963, 1968, 1971, 1972, 1973, 1975, 1977, 1995 by The Lockman Foundation.

Scripture marked MSG comes from The Message, Copyright © 1993, 1994, 1995, 1996, 2000, 2001, 2002 by Eugene H. Peterson.

Bible translations used are referenced at the back of the book.

Shelfie

A **free** eBook edition is available with the purchase of this print book.

CLEARLY PRINT YOUR NAME ABOVE IN UPPER CASE

Instructions to claim your free eBook edition:
1. Download the Shelfie app for Android or iOS
2. Write your name in **UPPER CASE** above
3. Use the Shelfie app to submit a photo
4. Download your eBook to any device

ISBN 978-1-63047-752-3 paperback
ISBN 978-1-63047-753-0 eBook
ISBN 978-1-63047-754-7 hardcover
Library of Congress Control Number:
2015913955

Cover Design by:
Rachel Lopez
www.r2cdesign.com

Interior Design by:
Bonnie Bushman
The Whole Caboodle Graphic Design

In an effort to support local communities and raise awareness and funds, Morgan James Publishing donates a percentage of all book sales for the life of each book to Habitat for Humanity Peninsula and Greater Williamsburg.

Get involved today, visit
www.MorganJamesBuilds.com

Habitat
for Humanity®
Peninsula and
Greater Williamsburg
Building Partner

To all who seek to experience God,
both in moments and in lives
empowered by and gratefully given over
to Him in worship.

"Praise the Lord, all you nations! Extol Him, all you peoples!"
—Psalm 117:1

"One of the greatest needs of the church is to develop worshippers."
—Ivan Veldhuizen, Executive Director of
International Ministries, Converge Worldwide

CONTENTS

Part 3: Surrendering to God

As we open ourselves to God, we realize He loves us deeply.

Part 4: Experiencing God

The essence of worship is to experience God and be changed.

Part 5: Living a Life of Worship

Our encounter with God leads to an everyday life of worship.

Epilogue: Life-Changing Worship

Isaiah's story teaches us about approaching God, surrendering to Him,
experiencing Him, and ultimately living life in a new way.

Preface

PERSPECTIVES

What Is Worship?

Ask twenty people what the word *worship* means, and you will get twenty different responses. Worship is a head-scratcher for those who don't go to church, a source of debate for many who do attend church, and a term of endearment for those who have experienced it in the deepest way.

For starters, worship is about God's worth much more than any event or activity we do. The modern English word worship comes from a phrase from the Middle Ages, worth-ship, which was used when addressing an English nobleman, lord, or king. The Bible declares God is "the King of kings and Lord of lords" and also tells us that God exists far above all the other so-called gods. It is in this context that the concept of "worth-ship" ultimately and infinitely applies to the One who was, and is, and is to come: God.

In this book, I present worship in the broadest sense of its definition because it is a multifaceted diamond given to us by God. At times I present worship as a deep, personal experience that compels us to respond. In other places, I explore the dimensions of worship that take place when we are together in worship with other people. Worship can involve scripture, music, silence, message, rituals, serendipitous moments, kneeling, standing, face-down-on-the-ground prayer, life stories, drama, listening, responding, life service, change, healing, and more.

But at its core, worship isn't about the things we do. Worship is the divine paradox that—while it involves doing—isn't focused on simply doing. In fact, we can go through the motions of worship and never really experience worship. God spoke of this in Isaiah 29 when He said the people worshipped Him with lip service but their hearts were far from Him. Worship is, at its heart, a state of being that is evidenced in many ways.

Authentic worship is about being a person whose life—every thought, word, and action—reflects and points to the ultimate "worth-ship" of God. Isaiah, a man who lived more than twenty-six hundred years ago, discovered this truth in a most amazing way.

Let's learn from Isaiah about living an everyday life of worship.

PART 1

WORSHIP

In worship we acknowledge our Mighty God with hearts of wonder and gratefulness, and we respond in a life of love, obedience, and service.

Chapter 1

FACE TO FACE

Have you ever met someone you always dreamed of meeting?

Happy Days

My story begins with the 1980s TV show *Happy Days*. It was one of my favorite programs as a teenager, but more important, it was also one of my wife's favorite programs. I always dreamed it would be cool to meet a TV actor, especially one from a classic show like *Happy Days*. I reasoned it probably never would happen, and even if it did, I might be disappointed by the experience. People rarely live up to their hype, or so I thought.

Let's fast-forward to St Paul, Minnesota, a few years ago.

I was invited to sing a song at a very large gala, a charitable event at a posh hotel. It was an upscale gathering, so much so that I had to rent a tuxedo (can we all say ex-PEN-sive?). I was more than a little nervous about singing in front of the huge crowd of business moguls, media stars, and influential people who populated the event.

When I arrived, I discovered that Marion Ross ("Mrs. C" from *Happy Days*) was also there, serving as honorary chair. She was seated in the front row as I ascended the platform to sing.

My nerves went off the chart at that point.

From what I remember of my performance, the song went well. After my song, I left the platform, and after a few minutes back stage, I tried to find Mrs. Ross. But she had already left the hall. A little disappointed, I made my way to the hotel lobby to leave.

And then it happened. Out of the blue this wonderful, gracious actress, along with her real-life husband, approached me. "Are you the young man who just sang that beautiful song?" she asked.

I thanked her for calling me young and told her yes, I was the one.

"You have a marvelous voice," she said and thanked me for my part in the night.

At that moment, I stirred up enough courage to tell her, "I know you've heard this a thousand times, but my wife and I are big fans of *Happy Days,* and we both love your work. Terese will be thrilled when I tell her I met you!"

Then she did something I will never forget. With her husband at her side, Marion Ross, "Mrs. C," took my hand, leaned over, and said, "Thank you . . . and please give this to your wife from me." Then she planted a kiss on my cheek.

I drove home on a cloud that night and excitedly told my wife every detail of what had happened. I also gave Terese the kiss Mrs. Ross instructed me to share. She was almost as excited as I was about the amazing encounter that night. It was a moment I will never forget.

Face to Face with God

Now imagine meeting *God* face to face—not some movie actor pretending to play God in a Hollywood movie, but the One who spoke His word and everything came into being. God!

Well, this is exactly what happened to a man named Isaiah. He lived about seven hundred years before Jesus Christ was born. Isaiah was born into a difficult and downward-spiraling time in the cultural and spiritual era of the Israelites. He was an Old Testament prophet whose words are still read and quoted today, thousands of years after his death. The book of Isaiah in the Bible is filled with visions and words that are both comforting and challenging, beautiful and stark, hopeful and harsh. It is a book that points to what God is about to do for His chosen people through a coming Messiah.

If Isaiah were interviewed today, he would emphatically state that the words He spoke came from God, not himself. He would insist his job was to faithfully listen to God and then accurately speak and do exactly as God instructed. The role of the Old Testament prophet was to be God's truth-teller to the people of his or her time, both leaders and regular citizens. Many scholars view Isaiah as the quintessential Old Testament prophet because he did just that.

The starting point of Isaiah's ministry was a spectacular event and vision in which Isaiah encounters God face to face, as described in the sixth chapter of the book of Isaiah. It gives us a picture of the beginning of Isaiah's new life calling and gives clues about what worship is all about.

It teaches us how to worship for a lifetime.

Chapter 2

ISAIAH'S VISION

H istory is filled with stories of leaders who began well but, after some success, succumbed to the consequences of poor personal spiritual and moral health. Isaiah lived when the once-great political leader King Uzziah was disqualified by God because of his spiritual and moral failures. When we witness people taken down by their bad behavior, loss of personal integrity, or lack of a spiritual and moral compass, the old saying still rings true: the more things change, the more they stay the same.

The Setting

This was the case as Isaiah vividly described his life-changing encounter with God. He told us it happened in the year King Uzziah died. As king of Judah, Uzziah started off well. His life and reign was highly successful and prosperous, primarily because of his unwavering heart, devotion, and obedience to God. But then Uzziah changed.

In the middle of his political and military successes, Uzziah started believing his own press and gave in to the temptations of pride and arrogance. Eventually he turned away from God and tried ruling Judah in his own way, apart from any reliance on the God of Abraham, Moses, and David, whom he once loved and served. The results of Uzziah's choices were disastrous. His legacy as king and the future of God's chosen people were forever scarred because of his prideful actions. He was afflicted with leprosy and spent his last days in isolation, wasting away from this dreaded and stigmatizing disease. The actions Uzziah took as a rogue king also set the scene for the eventual downfall of Jerusalem and destruction of the majestic temple Solomon had built hundreds of years earlier.

Add to this the growing pressure of external military threats from neighboring countries hell-bent on conquest, and you can understand this was no easy time to be alive. Even harder was being a prophet who had both hopeful and hard words from God to his people. The people of Israel had diluted and abandoned their commitment to their covenant relationship with God and had adopted religious and cultural practices of the surrounding peoples. This was not just some minor issue. These practices revealed the true state of their hearts. Just like their king, Uzziah, they had abandoned God in favor of themselves and the trendy, alluring worldviews that suited their desires.

This was the political and social backdrop for the divine experience Isaiah described when he stated he saw the Lord.

Isaiah's Vision

We don't know much about the nature of Isaiah's vision. It could have been a dream-like encounter or a literal transport to a different, heavenly realm. There are many instances in the Bible in which people encountered or heard from God in a dream. This could have been Isaiah's experience. In our time, there are many well-documented cases of near-death experiences that people describe as heaven-like encounters. It is possible Isaiah also had this type of experience in which he was whisked away to the heavenly realm.

Whatever the case, it is clear from Isaiah's description that this was a real, terrifying, and life-altering encounter with God. Isaiah found himself in a place different from anything he had experienced or imagined on planet earth.

The narration goes on to state that Isaiah saw the Lord God in all His unparalleled glory and majesty. God's beauty is so immense and pervasive that even the tail of His robe fills the heavenly temple with unimaginable glory. This was no mere deity that Isaiah could manipulate or coerce. Implied in Isaiah's description is that God sits above all things and all creatures and is in complete control of everything. He answers to no king, no power, or no one else. He is the beginning and the end. He *is* God, and Isaiah clearly knows it.

It's important to note that Isaiah tells us at this point he only *sees* the Lord (more on this in the next chapter) while *seeing* and *hearing* God's mighty angels, the Seraphim (translated as "burning ones"), who stood before God. Isaiah describes these powerful angels as being so in awe of God's holiness that they covered their faces and feet with their wings even as they soared on other wings of praise before God. These angels worshipped God and stood ready to move at His every command.

Isaiah describes hearing the angels tell each other about God in a three-fold worship song of God's holiness. Their voices shook the heavenly temple walls and floors to the foundation. Imagine the chest-pounding, earthquake-like tremor Isaiah must have felt at the sound of these angelic voices. The mighty Seraphim were so enthralled and captivated by God's beauty that they couldn't help telling each other about Him, and the heavenly sanctuary shook in resonance with their conversation. It was as if they were saying to each other, "Can you believe how wonderful and awesome God is? The Lord is so beautiful and magnificent that words fail us! Even as we thunder with all our voices, there is not enough praise to give Him! He is beyond comprehension!"

This was no forced or obligatory worship service. It was a heartfelt and spontaneous expression of love, awe, and devotion to the Great I Am.

Chapter 3

ISAIAH'S ENCOUNTER

After witnessing the perfect beauty of God in His eternal glory and hearing the angels' thunderous worship, Isaiah looked at himself and came to a sickening conclusion: he was as good as dead.

Because of the state of his filthy life and heart, Isaiah realized he deserved to be kicked out of God's beautiful presence. He also deserved death. He saw his pathetic faith, the pitifully lame excuse of his so-called worship of God, and he mourned out loud. He also grieved over the spiritual state of his fellow Israelites, whose worship of God was heartless and stale. He and his fellow humans deserved death because of this state of affairs, so Isaiah expected an imminent, painful "zap" of spiritual execution from one of God's angels.

But that isn't what he got.

A Burning Coal

Instead, one of these powerful angels went to the very altar of God and took a hot coal with a heavenly tong. It must have been extremely hot if even one of God's "flaming Seraphim" couldn't pick it up with angelic hands! Immediately the angel approached Isaiah and touched his tongue with the coal, telling him he was cleansed from his sin and guilt. Forgiven!

THE FIRE OF GOD

Read Leviticus 10:1–2.

During the exodus and time of wandering in the wilderness, the Israelites built a tabernacle according to God's plan and specifications. The altar of the tabernacle held God's holy fire. Aaron and his sons were set apart to minister to the Lord in this holy place. One day two sons of Aaron brought their own fire—against God's command—into the sanctuary. The result was devastating. The Bible states that "fire came out from the presence of the LORD and consumed them, and they died before the LORD."

The lesson: true cleansing comes from God, not from human efforts.

God's holiness and cleansing fire can't be manipulated or duplicated by people. It's important to understand that God is holy and cannot tolerate impure and arrogant attempts by people to get Him to do things their way.

As I reflect on this passage, it strikes me that what is important isn't only what is written, but what *isn't* written. An important clue is implied in this story, but to grasp it, we need to understand how the Seraphim operate.

The angel who approached Isaiah with the cleansing coal wasn't some rogue Seraphim distracted by Isaiah's presence, who then said to God, "Excuse me from reveling in your glory, but I'm going to take matters into my own hands and take care of this miserable, unclean human being. I'll get right back to you as soon as I'm finished with this guy."

Clearly that isn't what happened. We know from scriptures, such as Psalm 103:20, that God's angels act *only* on His direct command. Even in Isaiah's recounting of the events, he remembered the Seraphim referred to God as the "Commander of Heaven's armies."

My point is simple. The mighty Seraphim approached the altar of God, took a coal, and cleansed Isaiah *because* God ordered this heavenly being to do so! The angel, who worshipped God and stood ready to do what He bid him to do, acted only at the order of God Almighty. The incredible reality here is that Isaiah's cleansing came from God, through an angel who did exactly what God commanded.

God loved Isaiah so much He didn't want to see him destroyed but cleansed and made new. This says a lot about the character of God. God, who is holy and exists above and apart from everything in the cosmos, is also the same One who loves people beyond comprehension.

God loves us and longs to connect with us.

I believe Isaiah somehow understood this because he didn't resist the Seraphim coming his way or refuse to open his mouth to let the angel place an extremely hot coal on his tongue.

Isaiah simply surrendered to God.

Seeing and Hearing

But there is still one big, nagging question. If God loved Isaiah so much, why didn't Isaiah hear God giving the angel this order?

The answer comes in the telling conclusion of this story. Immediately after Isaiah was cleansed by God's purifying coal, he recounted the following:

"Then I heard the Lord."

Get that?

"Then I heard *the Lord"* (my emphasis).

It could be that up to this point, Isaiah could only see God's glory, but was able to see and hear the angels talking to each other. He may not have been able to hear God's voice because he wasn't clean. Isaiah was so dirty from his sin and the sin of his culture that he couldn't hear God's voice. The toxic junk of his life acted like earwax so that Isaiah was spiritually deaf to God until he was cleansed to hear His voice. Now that he was cleansed, his spiritual ears were finally attuned to God's voice.

And what was the first thing Isaiah heard God say?

Isaiah heard God ask for a willing volunteer. He recalled that God posed the question, *"Whom shall I send to the people of Israel, indeed to all people, to tell of my Character, my Glory, my Word, and my kingdom plan?"*

I'm convinced this was a rhetorical question. God already knew the answer. Isaiah's words, "Here am I. Send me," were more than just an impulsive, knee-jerk reaction from a hyper-emotional man. His "yes" response came from the heart of a man made clean and made brand new because God personally called him into His presence, cleansed him, and set a new life path in front of him. Isaiah's response was a personal act of worship—one that would span his lifetime.

After what Isaiah saw and heard, and after experiencing God firsthand, he couldn't help wanting to go and tell people about God. This call was burning in his heart more than the coal that had touched his tongue.

Send Me

"*Please* send me, God!" Isaiah cried out. And God said, "Yes."

Then God let Isaiah in on a troubling secret. Just as Isaiah couldn't hear God's voice even after seeing His glory and hearing the mighty Seraphim speak to each other, so the people to whom Isaiah would tell God's plans wouldn't be able to hear and see God, no matter what Isaiah said or did.

God told Isaiah in so many words, "You have to be OK with this working arrangement. You simply do what I tell you and let Me take care of the rest."

By saying yes to God, the die was cast for the rest of Isaiah's life. He knew this and agreed to God's plan. Why?

Isaiah not only saw and heard God, he met Him personally in a life-altering encounter. His life would never be the same. It couldn't be, not after meeting God face to face. His worship of God was purged of stale, lifeless crud and activated into a vibrant, every-day and every-moment reality.

For Isaiah, this was the beginning of a life of worship and service.

Chapter 4

LESSONS FROM ISAIAH

There are sixty-six chapters in the book of Isaiah. It is telling that Isaiah's vision took place toward the beginning of Isaiah's book (chapter 6) and not the end. I doubt the book of Isaiah would have existed if his enthusiastic response to God had faded and given way to life as usual. Thankfully, that isn't what happened. Isaiah's life trajectory and focus profoundly changed after his heavenly vision. The sixty chapters that follow this event are a testament to the fact that Isaiah's life and purpose was given to God as an act of worship. Isaiah didn't just worship God in one divine encounter. This event was one link in a long chain of Isaiah's lifelong commitment to worshipping and serving God.

Isaiah's life and ministry weren't easy by anyone's measure. Life for a prophet could be spiritually and physically hard and dangerous. Prophets were typically denigrated and mistreated, and Isaiah was no exception. Still, I can't help but think that the memory of Isaiah's meeting with God encouraged him and rekindled his passion during the hard days.

Isaiah's message to us is that worship is not just about an exciting, once-in-a-lifetime encounter with God, but it is about living each moment and each opportunity as a way of worshipping like the angels he had witnessed. His words and life spoke to his world, and still speak to us today, like the Seraphim he had heard: "Can you believe how wonderful and above everything God is? The Lord is so beautiful and magnificent that words fail us! Even as we thunder with all our voices, there is not enough praise to give Him! He is beyond comprehension."

So what does Isaiah's story have to do with us today?

Approaching, Surrendering, Experiencing, Activating

I see four foundational lessons we can learn from Isaiah about truly worshipping God.

1. Approaching God in Worship
   - God is the initiator of the worship process. He is the One who invites us to approach Him in worship, regardless of our social status, past accomplishments or failures, our strengths and faults. Ultimately God desires a heart-to-heart encounter, not some arm's-length pretense of worship that is not real and meaningful.
   - As we enter into worship, we see God's glory evidenced in who He is, what He has created, and in others who are experiencing Him firsthand.
   - As we approach God in worship, we come with no other agenda except awe, amazement, and gratefulness towards Him.
   - We then arrive at the honest realization of our inadequacy before Him. Like Isaiah, we are people with unsightly spiritual garbage inside us, and wherever we live on

earth, we live in a culture that is toxic as well. Honestly acknowledging that reality opens us to receive God's burning love and forgiveness.

2. Surrendering Ourselves to God
   - As we open ourselves to God, we realize He loves us deeply and doesn't want us to stay where we are spiritually or stay where we are in life. He wants to touch us, change us, and bring us to a better place through worship.
   - God asks us to willingly and continually surrender ourselves to Him and His forgiveness, cleansing power, and grace. Even as we yield to God, we recognize that healing and grace come only from God's hand, not our efforts.

3. Experiencing God
   - The essence of worship is to experience God and be changed in this encounter, both in our personal time with God and when we gather with others in God-directed and empowered worship.
   - When we experience God, we are filled with the energy and desire to live more and more for Him. Like Isaiah, we raise our hand and passionately exclaim, "Here I am. Send me!"

4. Activating a Living Worship
   - Our worship encounter with God is confirmed and activated as we respond to His call to do His kingdom work on earth and live each day and moment as an act of worship for Him.

Isaiah's story can teach us a lot about approaching God, surrendering to Him, experiencing Him, and ultimately living life in a new way because of an encounter with God. His response to God is the essence of what it means to worship God.

Let's consider each of these lessons from Isaiah.

Chapter 5

DEFINING WORSHIP

Why Worship?

"W hy did God create worship?"

This was a question I asked thirty people, mainly pastors, at a course I recently taught on worship. One student later told me he thought this was the most important question he had ever heard on the subject of worship.

There were lots of great responses centering on the fact that we are created to worship God to give Him glory—which is true—along with other theologically sound answers. Yet, I challenged them, could there be an even deeper answer to the question of why God made this thing we call worship?

Case in point: At one point, as Jesus was entering Jerusalem, the religious leaders of His time tried to order Him to silence the people who were vibrantly and vocally worshipping Him as God's promised One, the Messiah. Jesus's response to the religious leaders was that even if those who were worshipping Him became silent, the very rocks around them would cry out in worship (Luke 21:37–40). His point is that no person can silence the praise of creation toward its Creator. We hear it in radio waves that sing from distant stars, drum-roll rumblings from distant thunderstorms, and the rhythmic crashes of ocean waves.

I hate to burst our self-important bubble, but also implied in Jesus's words is that God doesn't need human worship to be validated, happy, or loved.

For starters, God is the self-sufficient and all-powerful One and is the only One who is! God exists in a perfect, harmonious, unending, and unbending love relationship as the Father, Son, and Holy Spirit.

Second, the entire cosmos sings and dances in worship to God. God's creation points both to His beauty and His awesome, unequalled power. It cannot help but speak out with sights, sounds, smells, and textures to the One who spoke everything into being and holds everything together to this day and past whenever the end of the current cosmos comes.

Finally, far too many people—consciously or not— perceive worship as a way to get God to see and do things our way. I've been guilty of this more than a few times in my life. We say the right words and even convince ourselves that we are worshipping God, but in our innermost being, we still want to be in control, and we perceive God as the means to our own ends. The religious leaders of Jesus's day were also guilty of this. They wanted religious decorum and personal power, not God. In fact, they didn't even recognize God in the person of Jesus Christ, though He was right before their eyes.

God doesn't need our worship. Then WHY did He ordain and create worship?

The only explanation I can think of is that God intensely loves us, so much so that He wants us to *intimately* experience His presence, love, and transforming power in our being, lives, circumstances, and world. His love is so great that He created a way for us to intimately and powerfully experience Him and His love SO THAT we can be transformed into all He created us to be. He not only made us to worship Him voluntarily, but he also made worship FOR us to come to Him and experience Him deeply.

Because we are free to worship God—or not—real worship requires a voluntary, day-to-day decision on our part to truly want to approach God for who He really is, submit to Him, experience Him, and then live in Him and for Him. When we take the focus off ourselves and put it onto God, He opens the door for us to come and meet with Him, know Him, and experience all His is.

Worship isn't a mere theological exercise or existential religious chess game. Authentic worship is the most important reason for our lives. Real worship can only happen through the person of Jesus Christ, in the power of the Holy Spirit. When we stop putting ourselves at the center of the universe and focus our being on God who IS the center, we come away deeply satisfied—regardless of our current external conditions, good or bad.

God doesn't need our worship—but He WANTS our worship because He is deeply in love with you and me and wants us to experience Him and His deep love and transforming power.

Defining Worship

Authentic worship transcends merely going through religious activities or rituals. Worship comes alive when God becomes the very breath of our being, the true desire of our heart, the object of our thoughts, and the movement of our life. Worship is about acknowledging God for who He is and about responding to Him.

In worship we acknowledge our Mighty God with hearts of Wonder and Gratefulness, and we respond in a life of love, obedience, and service.

William Temple once described worship as "the submission of all our nature to God. It is the quickening of conscience by His holiness; the nourishment of mind with His truth; the purifying of imagination by His Beauty; the opening of the heart to His love; the surrender of will to His purpose—and all of this gathered up in adoration, the most selfless emotion of which our nature is capable and therefore the chief remedy for that self-centeredness which is our original sin and the source of all actual sin" (William Temple's "Readings in St. John's Gospel").

Worship at the deepest level does the following:

- Acknowledges God at the very core of our being (It connects us with God in heart, mind, soul, and body.)
- Fixes our minds and hearts on Jesus Christ as we increasingly become God-conscious, rather than self-conscious
- Unleashes the work of the Holy Spirit in and through us
- Reflects God's Word
- Expresses authenticity and truth
- Happens on a personal level (It's real and personal.)
- Is shared and experienced with other Christ-followers
- Engages us with God and draws us closer to Him
- Is life-yielding (We give ourselves to God.)
- Is life-changing (We come away different, moving from glory to glory.)

God is asking you and me to enter into the same worship experience that Isaiah knew: ***approaching***, ***surrendering***, ***experiencing***, and ***activating*** our worship of God—not just for a moment, but throughout life and into eternity. It's worship for a lifetime.

———— Reflections on Worship ————

In worship, we acknowledge our Mighty God with hearts of wonder and gratefulness, and we respond in a life of love, obedience, and service.

Perspectives

What are your first-thought reflections on Isaiah's experience with God (Isaiah 6)? What strikes you as important, interesting, or challenging?

Foundations

Going into this study, what were your concepts on worship? How would you define worship?

Insights

In worship we acknowledge our mighty God . . . and we respond.

What are your thoughts about worship foundationally being about acknowledging and responding to God's worthiness?

How did Isaiah differ from King Uzziah in his attitude about himself? How did Isaiah avoid this downfall? How can we avoid this attitude in our world today?

How do you respond to the insights about approaching, surrendering, experiencing, and living a life of worship?

Application

Isaiah saw himself and his sin, and he anticipated his fate. Then God offered him cleansing. How do you see your sinful self before God? How do you receive His cleansing?

How do you see Part 1's "Worship" insights? Are they challenging? Do they change or reinforce your perspectives and experience? How might you apply this?

PART 2

APPROACHING GOD IN WORSHIP

God calls us to a heart-to-heart encounter.

As we enter into worship, we see God's glory evidenced in who He is, what He has created, and in others who are experiencing Him firsthand.

As we approach God in worship, we come with no other agenda but awe, amazement, and gratefulness.

Chapter 6

GOD'S GREATNESS: THE SCALE, PART 1

saiah's story teaches us some important lessons about worship, whether we come before Him alone or with other people who are in a relationship with Christ. The first lesson from Isaiah on how to approach God is what I call "the balance of the scale."

Think about a balancing scale, one that is often referred to as the scale of justice. The two opposing sides must come together in perfect harmony in order to maintain a precise balance. There is a similar balance needed as we approach  God in worship. When we discover this balance, we can be released from the bonds of human understanding and can soar with God in worship. Let's look at the scale from the perspective of each side, beginning with this verse from Hebrews:

> Therefore since we are receiving a kingdom that cannot be shaken, let us be thankful, and so worship God acceptably with reverence and fear. (Heb.12:28)

It's very tempting to try to put God in a mental "box" of our own creation. We humans are wired to see, feel, touch, taste, and wrap our minds around a picture of something or someone so that we can better relate to it—or maybe even have a measure of control over it. We're also inclined to wrestle with and sort things out. So naturally we want to try to "figure out" the important questions of our life: "Who is God?" "What does He look like?" "What is His ultimate agenda?"

The biggest, most fundamental question is both simple and unsettling: "How do I define God, who is beyond definition?" God's answer to Moses when He was asked to define Himself by name was both simple and incomprehensible: "I AM who I AM."

I AM who I AM. What does this mean? I don't think anyone other than Jesus Christ can fully answer this question. As finite human beings, we must face the fact that we will never be able to fully comprehend the depth of an infinite God. I believe we will spend eternity in amazed wonder as God continues to reveal more and more of Himself to us. The implications of this acceptance mean we need to let go of our efforts to put God in our box and instead enter into the uncertainty that He is so far above us that our attempts to define Him fall flat.

The truth is God is above both time and space. He is eternal. Reflect on that: God is sovereign over everything, including time and space, so He is not affected by or subject to either. He is beyond the beginning, exists beyond the ending, and is limitless everywhere in between. To

God, everything is within Him and every time is *now*. There is no matter (or anti-matter!) that controls Him. Space and time dimensions are subject to Him. Light-years and distances are irrelevant to Him, simply because He *is*. It is hard for us to comprehend this because we live in linear time with a beginning and ending in a well-defined space.

But consider the universe for a moment. Scientists speculate that it is at least 156 billion light-years wide. That means it would take billions of years traveling at the speed of light to travel the width (not the length) of the universe. At this point in history, humans haven't been able to travel at the speed of light, and even if we could, it would still take more time than the human race has been on this planet to travel across the universe. And yet God is bigger than this. He exists above and beyond the cosmos He created by speaking it into being.

We also see the power of the universe, with stars consuming planets and other suns and with volcanoes erupting and spewing out fire and molten material that consumes anything in its path and makes new land. God is also about the work of restoring a broken cosmos, and this means He will use His holy fire to consume the broken old and forge His perfect new kingdom.

The universe is God's handiwork, so its unfathomable vastness, elegant symmetry, diverse wonder, and even frightening dynamics can point us to His nature and power. The apostle Paul put it this way:

For since the creation of the world God's invisible qualities—his eternal power and divine nature—have been clearly seen, being understood from what has been made, so that people are without excuse. (Rom 1:20)

The stark reality is that He alone is God, and we are beautiful-yet-flawed specks of created, animated dust in the cosmos. Now reflect on the scripture passage we began with: "Our God is a consuming fire" (Heb. 12:28). If this doesn't evoke a twinge of awe and fear of God and His power, read this section again, and ask God to help you experience the gravity of who He is. When we embrace this, we will worship God as Isaiah did when he said, "Woe to me. I am ruined! For I am a man of unclean lips, and I live among a people of unclean lips, and my eyes have seen the King, the Lord Almighty." God's inestimable power leads us to see who we really are in the light of who God really is!

In his story, Isaiah described feeling the immense weight of God's infinite power and majesty. It was a weight that almost crushed him until he experienced the other side of the scale of worshipping God: God's love.

Chapter 7

GOD'S LOVE:
THE SCALE, PART 2

The first side of the "scale" of worship is weighted with the awareness that God is God and we are not. When we fully grasp that His vastness and being are so far beyond us, we will be led to bow our hearts, minds, and beings before Him. But the worship scale is also equally balanced by the weight of this scripture:

See what great love the Father has lavished on us, that we should be called children of God! And that is what we are! (1 John 3:1)

A pastor friend recently reminded me that this infinitely big God, The Great I AM, chose to become a human embryo smaller than the dot inside this parenthesis: (.). That is the size of an early human embryo.

God did this out of crazy, infinite love for you and me.

GOD'S COMPASSION
Read Psalm 103:8–12.

God's glorious love balances His awesome, terrifying power with immense patience and compassion. Consider the universe God spoke into being: scientists speculate that it is at least 156 billion light-years wide! The same God whose power flung the universe into place offers people His grace and forgiveness.

The lesson: When we say yes to God, He gives us His grace and forgiveness. Our sins are forever put away from us, farther than the length of the universe!

The worship scale is counterweighted with the experiential knowledge that God left his eternal position and became a real man in the person of Jesus of Nazareth. In Jesus, God Himself paid the ultimate price of death for our flawed and tarnished being so that we can have a new, perfect, and eternal Father-child relationship with God. Regardless of our past or present, God loves us and invites us to come to Him.

Isaiah experienced this when the angel came to him with the burning coal, not to execute him but to cleanse him so that he could experience God himself.

God in the flesh. It's a hard thing to wrap our minds around because it is beyond our limited human comprehension that God could come as a human being to save us. But it's true. God, in the person of Jesus Christ, was conceived by the power of God's Holy Spirit in the person of Mary, lived a totally flawless life, spoke and taught in eternal union with the Father, and then somehow, incredibly, took our every flaw, weakness, and sin to the cross to pay the required price for our broken nature and sinful choices. Jesus rose again and is alive today and will come again soon to complete God's kingdom plan on earth, just as it is in heaven.

The next time you think about Jesus on the cross, remember that God the Father lives above and beyond time and space, so His eternal experience of Jesus's death on the cross is now, more than just remembering a historical event that occurred some two thousand years ago in our linear understanding of life. God experiences His son's death and resurrection *now*, even as you read this sentence. He chose this because it was the only way you and I could be saved. He did this out of an unfathomable and perfect love for you and me.

Through Jesus, God gave you and me the opportunity to be his new, *adopted* children, for now and throughout eternity. The Bible says that to all who say yes to God through the person of Jesus Christ, we become "co-heirs" with Christ to everything the Father has given to Him. Jesus is not only our Redeemer, He is also our "first born" (Rom. 8:28) and most-favored older brother. We will someday even inherit resurrected bodies just like His.

God is not like all imperfect human dads, but a loving Abba-Daddy who longs and searches to hug us, hold us, take care of us, and give us Himself and everything else He knows we need. It's almost harder for us to understand God's infinite love for each of us than it is to comprehend His tremendous power.

As for me, I choose to receive God's love as a total and free gift, and nothing I have ever done, am doing, or will ever do could make the slightest dent in paying Him back for it. I don't deserve it, but God has called me and made me his eternally loved child. When I embrace this truth, I am compelled to sit at Jesus's feet and worship Him with utter love and abandon for all He is and all He has done for me.

So this is the delicate balance for you to discover and experience:

- On one side, God's incomparable, awesome, frightening power and holiness.
- On the other side, God's undeserved and never-ending love for you and me.

When we personally approach God with this delicate balance in mind, we will soar with God and overcome the gravity of human bonds as we worship Him.

Chapter 8

HATS AND CROWNS

Hats

Hats are interesting things. As I walked down a street in Orlando, Florida, recently, I observed an amazing assortment of headwear on display as people walked through a sunny, sticky day. One twenty-something was wearing a knit skullcap. Others had baseball caps that advertised their allegiance to a particular team, beach, or city. A few women had wide-brimmed hats, while other people wore hats that marked their employment as a bus driver or police officer. Hats identify people's passions, occupations, and more.

The Bible is silent on what Isaiah was wearing when he entered into the heavenly vision. It seems almost ridiculous to even ask what Isaiah was wearing in light of the magnitude of what he experienced. But there is still a lesson for us to learn from what Isaiah didn't wear in his heavenly encounter. Whether we realize it or not, we sometimes wear attitude "hats" when we approach God, whether we worship Him alone or with other people.

One particularly dangerous attitude hat we wear has the word *consumerism* embroidered on it. Our culture has ingrained in us the notion that we deserve to get something out of everyone and everything we come across. Sadly, this flawed mindset can work its way into our attitude about worshipping God. When we wear the hat of the consumer, we focus only on what will we get out of worship, rather than what will we give to God in worship.

I need to qualify this a bit. There are times when we are so deep in the valley of life's hardships that all we can do is cry out to God. This is a good thing and part of an authentic interaction with God in worship. This is not the consumer mentality I am talking about.

The worship consumerism I am addressing is the, Jabba-the-Hut type of attitude in which we come to a worship experience already fat in our own self-centeredness, only to demand from God and others that we get fed more to appease our own appetite, rather than focus on and give authentic worship to God.

There is also the danger of entering worship in the presence of other people with a critical attitude that demands the message, worship music, or other elements of worship fit our personal expectations and tastes. This approach assumes we know better than the pastor, worship planners, or anyone else what is best. Isaiah would counsel those with this attitude to instead come to worship Jesus Christ with a humble heart that longs to meet with Him.

There is also the temptation to approach worship as the way to get God to do things our way. It is the "if-then" approach: *if* I appease God in worship . . . *then* He will do what I want.

This is exactly how the pagans in the first century approached the idols and gods of their day: get their attention; appease them, so that they will grant us prosperity, fertility, or whatever else we desire.

It was a misguided and flawed approach to life. It simply doesn't work. Yet some still try this with God today.

Don't get me wrong. God loves us and promises to take care of us and provide for our needs. But God does this in the context of us having Him as our first and only heart's desire, not having the stuff He gives to us as primary.

Think about it. If we really believe we can manipulate God, we are falsely believing we are more clever or knowledgeable than God—which is ridiculous. When we accept this mode of thinking, we unconsciously make ourselves into false gods, and our desires become more important than meeting with God. This is the very definition of idol worship. Isaiah warned the people of Israel about self-centered worship when he reported what God said:

These people come near to me with their mouth and honor me with their lips, but their hearts are far from me. Their worship of me is based on merely human rules they have been taught. (Is. 29:13)

It's interesting that Isaiah never asked, "What's in it for me?" when he was drawn into God's presence in the heavenly worship experience. With no personal agenda, Isaiah was able to experience God and all His glory.

Crowns

There is another powerful illustration of hats in the Bible. This is another moving illustration of what it looks like to worship God unencumbered by agendas.

The book of Revelation, the last book in the Bible, has a revealing and beautiful picture of the worship experience in heaven. In this scene, the twenty-four elders, pictured as before the throne of God, are arrayed in the pure, white garments of salvation and righteousness that comes from Christ alone. Most Scripture scholars maintain that the twenty-four elders represent the church, those people who have encountered Jesus Christ and given their hearts, lives, and allegiance to Him alone. It's important to see that these elders are also wearing gold crowns, the symbol of being adopted as sons and daughters of the King, with all the authority and honor royalty carries. Watch carefully what happens as they approach God in worship:

> The twenty-four elders fall down before him who sits on the throne, and worship him who lives for ever and ever. They lay their crowns before the throne and say: You are worthy, our Lord and God, to receive glory and honor and power, for you created all things, and by your will they were created and have their being. (Rev. 4:10–11)

I believe this is the picture of how we are to approach God in worship. Let's break down their approach to worshipping God.

First, the elders display a stirring posture of humility and awe as we see them fall before God. The utter majesty and extreme power of God's presence makes them weak in the knees.

Next, they take off their crowns. This is the heartfelt sign and statement before God that there is nothing we have ever done to deserve our new, all-is-well relationship with Him. We are nothing apart from God, and our righteous position before Him is only because of His magnificent love and work on our behalf. All our so-called accomplishments, privileges, and status are worthless compared to Him.

Finally, the words they voice flow from the depth of their being: God alone deserves all the fame, respect, honor, power, and worship we can give Him because He is God, the author and ruler of everything. It's not a dry, doctrinal statement of belief, but an overwhelming love song to God.

This heart-orientation and mindset go against our human nature. We can't achieve this by trying harder on our own. To do so is simply a formula for failure. To experience the kind of worship we were made to know can only happen by God's divine intervention in the very depths of our being. Today, ask God to infuse you with the same heart for worshipping Him that Isaiah and the elders around the throne experienced.

Chapter 9

SACRED PLACE

A colleague who is a pastoral counselor recently returned from a national conference for his profession. He told me it was reported at this conference that scientists have found a place in our brain in which a single photon starts firing rapidly at the onset of one single thought. The word that initiates this response is *God*. Studies have shown that when a person starts thinking about God, there is a specific place in the brain that begins sparking in response. As a person of faith, this makes sense to me because I believe every human being is hardwired to connect with God. The only question is if and when each of us chooses to activate this process.

Imagine how different our lives would look (as well as our marriages, families, communities, and world) if there were daily, internal sparks firing in the most important relationship of our lives: our life with God.

Isaiah had a strong desire to meet God. I can't help but wonder if his heavenly visit flowed out of a time and place Isaiah had determined to keep because he wanted to encounter Him in the deepest way.

The starting point of a dynamic and spark-filled life of worship happens when we make the decision to meet with God every day—regardless of our circumstances, perceived abilities or lack of abilities, schedules, or obstacles. I know from personal experience that the obstacles and distractions to meeting God can be numerous and daunting: frenetic households, sick or crying kids, pressing work schedules, assignments to do, and much more. You probably also will feel awkward and prayer-challenged as you start on this new journey of worship. That's okay. Begin by asking God to teach and help you as you commit to meet with Him. Remember, He loves to reveal Himself to people who diligently seek Him.

I intentionally stated that setting a time to meet with God is "the starting point of a dynamic and spark-filled worship life" because the decision to meet God daily doesn't necessarily guarantee that we will actually worship God. There is always the danger that our daily time with God can turn into a legalistic or formulaic exercise, rather a life-changing time of entering into the presence of God.

However, the fear of this happening shouldn't prevent us from making the decision to spend time in God's presence daily.

The importance of choosing to worship God on a personal basis begins by making time to meet with Him. Jesus did this. The Bible tells us He regularly went off to a solitary place to be with God in prayer (Luke 5:16). When you think about it, cultivating a healthy relationship always involves making conscious choices to get together. My wife Terese and I have found that the lunch and dinner dates we regularly schedule with each other are strong investments in our marriage. During these dates, we get to know each other better. We also find they add more spark to our relationship.

Once you've committed yourself to meet God daily, finding a time and place to connect with Him is not only important but also uniquely personal. The question is, "Where do you find a sacred place, and what does it look like?"

The definition of the word sacred is "to set apart or dedicate to God." A sacred place is anywhere we set apart to go and meet God: a desk, car, a trail, lawn chair, easy chair—you name it.

Here are some examples:

- Moses first encountered God in the burning bush found in the mountainous area of a desert that likely smelled like the sheep he was tending in his job as a shepherd (Exodus 3). Because He was there, God told Moses the place he met Him was "holy ground."
- Daniel worshipped in his upstairs room with the windows wide open, in a country where worshipping God meant a death sentence (Daniel 6).
- Paul and Silas, falsely accused, beaten, and imprisoned, made the choice to worship God in the squalid, noisy prison, in which they found themselves shackled, in the middle of the night (Acts 16:25–34).
- Jesus often went to a solitary place in order to spend time with God the Father, including the night before His death on the cross.

In all these instances, their worship experience gave way to a mighty work of God that profoundly affected the world. The sparks of God's power were flying.

I can't tell you where or when to meet God. I can't guarantee that every meeting with God will be like Isaiah's experience in the Most Sacred place. My only advice is to find a time and/or place where you can meet with God uninterrupted; then spend time with Him. It made a world of difference to Isaiah, and it can for you as well.

Chapter 10

APPROACHING WITH OTHERS

G od didn't wire us to be "lone ranger" worshippers. We are made to worship God in the presence of other authentic Christ-followers. Isaiah witnessed a community of mighty Seraphim worshipping God, and he was ushered into experiencing God in the context of that worship. The Bible also tells us that one day we will join with countless others in extraordinary worship, centered around God the Father, Son, and Holy Spirit.

We call the presence of two or more Christ-followers different names: "the church," "the body of Christ," "the bride of Christ," "believers," "brothers and sisters in Christ," "followers of the Way," and more. The underlying reality of the church is that the same Lord Jesus Christ who lives in other people calls us to join them in living and experiencing God together. The gathering of the church (God's people) in worship is a God-designed thing. There is nothing better on this earth than when authentic worship takes place among believers (see 1 Corinthians 14:25).

As a leader, I live for the moments when the church comes ready to give God whole-hearted, life-evidenced worship. In these moments, I have seen hardened people softened, hopeless people encouraged, wounded people healed, and the church set aglow by the presence of Almighty God in our midst.

Even in our new nature as Christ-followers, we still struggle with our humanity, so sometimes worship can become a dull, empty ritual. As we acknowledge this reality, we need to own our part in it and remind ourselves that God's "worth-ship" deserves much better than this. If we honestly evaluate ourselves, we will see that at times we have let our personal preferences and attitudes infiltrate the collective worship experience of the church. This is the opposite of worship, because *our* needs become the real focus, not God.

Worship among believers requires a measure of sacrifice, especially among the more mature in faith, so that God is supremely honored above our desires and expectations. This requires mature faith in God and a steadfast focus on His kingdom plans.

For example, consider your music preferences in worship. As a worship leader, I frequently receive feedback on music selections and styles. This may be an appeal or critique regarding the selection of traditional hymns or current worship songs. While I regard this feedback as helpful, I often share this insight: Probably a third of the songs I lead are not my personal favorites. However, God has taught me I can offer these songs as my own "sacrifice of praise" because they are bringing someone else into the presence of God. When I began to practice this, God brought me a new depth of meaning and a new love for the songs I wouldn't necessarily choose on my own. It helped me recognize worship is about engaging and approaching God with others.

One of the amazing paradoxes of worship is sacrifice. When we sacrifice something we cherish for God's sake, we gain infinitely more: His very presence. Furthermore, worship and sacrifice are inextricably linked in the Bible:

> Through Jesus, therefore, let us continually offer to God a sacrifice of praise—the fruit of lips that confess his name. (Heb. 13:15)

The dictionary defines sacrifice as "the surrender or destruction of something prized for the sake of something considered as having a higher or more pressing claim."

Baseball players know about sacrifice. They are often asked to give up a chance to get on base so that another runner can advance or score. They do this because the greater reward—winning the game—is more important than their personal achievement. Imagine how powerful the church would be if more Christians were willing to sacrifice personal preferences in the context of worship for the greater good of God's kingdom. I am convinced worship would become even more greatly filled with His presence.

"We bring the sacrifice of praise into the house of the Lord" is an old song that has been a standard in many churches. I remember hearing and singing this song when I was young. One day, as I sang it, this thought occurred to me: "Do we really understand what we are singing? Are we prepared to put to death our preferences and expectations for sacrificial worship that puts God first? Are we ready to give God sacrificial worship that demands a personal cost from us?"

The primary question as we enter worship is this: "Who are we really here to please when we come to worship?" If the answer to this question is *me*, then any sacrifice is too much. If the answer to this question is *God,* then personal sacrifice in worship becomes our joyful gift to Him.

As you approach God in worship today, ask Him to create in you a heart that looks at sacrifice as a privilege to offer Him, in light of the enormous personal sacrifice God gave for you in Jesus Christ.

—— **Reflections on Approaching God in Worship** ——

God calls us to a heart-to-heart encounter.

Perspectives

What are your first-thought perspectives and reflections on approaching God in worship? What strikes you as important, interesting, or challenging?

Foundations

Have you ever met someone famous or powerful? How did you feel? Imagine yourself approaching God in heaven's throne room. How would it differ?

When and how do you approach God by yourself? What helps you come into God's presence with an open heart?

What are some attitude "hats" we can wear into worship? How might we sometimes approach as a consumer or critic, or with another perspective?

Insights

As we enter into worship, we see God's glory evidenced in who He is, what He has created, and in others who are experiencing Him firsthand. As we approach God in worship, we come with no other agenda but awe, amazement, and gratefulness.

Our Christian faith is distinguished in acknowledging our all-powerful Creator God who also has such personal love for each of us. How do you respond to God's greatness and love?

Paul speaks of an unbeliever coming into the gathering of believers and being convicted by the presence of God (1 Cor. 14:24-25). What does a worship service need to be like for this kind of experience today?

Application

How do you see Part 2's "Approaching" insights as challenging, changing, or reinforcing your perspectives and experience? How are you being called closer to God in worship?

How might you apply this?

PART 3

SURRENDERING TO GOD

As we open ourselves to God, we realize He loves us deeply.

He wants to touch us, change us, and bring us to a better place through worship. God asks us to willingly and continually surrender ourselves to Him and to His forgiveness, power, and grace.

Even as we yield to God, we recognize healing and grace come only from God's hand, not our efforts.

Chapter 11

YIELD

Have you noticed that fewer people are yielding to other cars on the road these days? Our roads have become a battlefield of every person for himself. In the breakneck pace of traffic on our streets and freeways, the word *yield* has become associated with weakness or capitulation. Legally, when we see the yield sign, we are expected to defer to other traffic. We are to look and wait until the proper time when we can move without violating the right of way of other drivers, bikers, and walkers. However, yielding seems to be more the exception than the rule in our society. In my home state, drivers are supposed to stop whenever someone enters a crosswalk. But I have lost count of the times I've seen pedestrians wait or even jump out of the way because some driver blew through a legal crosswalk.

Why is this happening? I am convinced that yielding goes against our human nature. External laws of yielding fizzle without the motive to yield, either by threat of a ticket or the inner desire to obey the traffic laws. The act of yielding can especially grate against us when we need to get somewhere and someone else momentarily controls our destiny. We want to be in control of our destiny, and yielding can feel like weakness. Truth be told, we've all known this feeling. I know I have.

A Paradox

It's a paradox that the same word, yielding, that symbolizes weakness to many people is also the key to experiencing God's power and strength in our life. The turning point of Isaiah's heavenly visit came when he yielded his tongue to the hot coal the angel brought from God's holy altar. Isaiah knew he was yielding himself not to some angel, but to God Himself. Make no mistake about it, yielding is both an important component and indicator of an authentic life of worship.

Jesus is not only *the* perfect model of a life totally yielded to God, He is the One who enables and equips us to yield to God. He constantly reminded people that His purpose was to glorify God the Father and not Himself. His is the very definition of a yielded life of worship:

[Jesus], being in very nature God, did not consider equality with God something to be used to his own advantage; rather, he made himself nothing by taking the very nature of a servant, being made in human likeness. And being found in appearance as a man, he humbled himself by becoming obedient to death—even death on a cross! (Phil. 2:5–8)

Jesus yielded Himself totally to God the Father and His plan, with no thought of personal gain or power. He showed us a perfectly yielded life. But how can we ever do what Jesus did? Yielding and submitting ourselves to God is a good indicator that worship has moved from the realm of the theoretical into a new, God-empowered reality.

But yielding is hard. Most likely, while driving you have had someone suddenly cut in front of you. The problem is that our natural reaction to this event is to be offended—and sometimes even become offensive—because someone has violated our rights on the road.

The point of this illustration is simply that circumstances can present serious challenges to the life we want to live as an act of worship to God. Putting other people first and yielding to the interests and needs of others instead of demanding our own way—we simply cannot do any of this through our human strength or striving.

But How?

If yielding goes against our very nature, how can we possibly yield to God as an act of worship?

We can't, at least not by our own efforts. The beautiful irony of yielding is this: We simply ask God to empower us to yield to Him through His Holy Spirit and Word. We start with the simple prayer and decision to yield ourselves to God, just as Isaiah did. Until this is the real prayer of our heart, anything else we do is meaningless.

There is one word in Colossians 3 that is the key to overcoming the challenges that life often throws at us. It is the word *let*:

Let the peace of Christ rule in your hearts, since as members of one body you were called to peace . . . Let the message of Christ dwell among you richly. (verses 15–17)

The dictionary defines let as meaning "allow." Allow is defined as "to give permission."

Only God can empower us to be able to put the interests of others above our own—provided we ask Him and yield ourselves to His touch. This holds true in our families, friendships, work associations, schools, churches, worship services, and especially as we witness to other people through our lives (including our driving attitudes and behaviors).

In order to experience a dynamic life given in worship to God, we must continually give permission for Christ's peace (that is, His presence) to *rule* or control the very core of our being. This is the life-altering alternative to *me* being in control and making all the decisions on how I will act or react. God won't ever impose His rule on us, but instead, He tells us to make decisions of our will to yield to Him, time and time again. It's not enough for Jesus to be in the mixing pot of our life with all the other stuff we cherish. He wants to be the director in charge of everything that comes in and goes out of us. This is what "submitting to God" means, and we all know at times it isn't easy to do. Submission goes against the grain of human nature, against our culture, and against the strong pull to "be my own boss." It seems an impossible task. But the Bible tells us all things are possible for God.

Yielding to God and letting God rule in our life is the core response of authentic worship.

Yielding and Deferring

There is another key *let* in this passage: "Let the message of God dwell in you richly." If we take the time to understand this verse, we will see that God is offering us the most powerful tool—His living Word—to see victory happen in our lives and in our churches. We are told to make the conscious decision to allow His Word into our minds and hearts, and even to allow it to live abundantly in us. It's the spiritual equivalent of the phrase, "You are what you eat," because the more we take in God's Word, the more it transforms the fabric of our being. When a steady diet of consuming God's Word is energized by the power of Jesus Christ ruling inside us, then we will see big changes happening in us: exciting, take-your-breath-away changes that will look and feel like miracles.

When this prayer becomes the cry of our heart, there are several ways the prayer begins to be answered in our life.

First, we actively **yield to God** over our thoughts, inclinations, and plans. Paul writes in 2 Corinthians 10:5 that we are to "take every thought captive" to Christ. Pause for a moment and think about this: what does yielding even the tiniest thought to God mean? Not only does this cut off false ideas and temptations from taking root in our lives, it also opens a conduit for us to experience the "mind of Christ." We literally yield and open ourselves to God's unimaginable wisdom.

Second, we yield and **defer to other people** over our interests and agenda. This is a key theme that the Apostle Paul presented to the churches of the New Testament and to us. Check out these verses:

Submit to one another out of reverence for Christ. (Eph. 5:21)

Do nothing out of selfish ambition or vain conceit. Rather, in humility value others above yourselves, not looking to your own interests but each of you to the interests of the others. In your relationships with one another, have the same mindset as Christ Jesus. (Phil. 2:3–5)

Finally, there are real-life church applications to these two "let components." Submitting isn't intended as action for us as individuals only; it is meant to be the growing reality in our churches. I have witnessed church-fracturing disputes about worship services (especially in areas of music and preaching styles) that the enemy has used to diminish or curtail the kingdom-effectiveness of churches. If you struggle with this, it might be good to pray about and reflect on these questions:

- Do I honestly seek Christ to rule in my heart and church over my personal preferences?
- Do I allow God's Word and Spirit to lead me to love those who see things differently than I do?
- Do I look for ways to pray for and build up other people, and so witness to them that my attitudes and behaviors are Word- and Spirit-controlled?
- Do I humble myself to submit to what God-placed leadership has prayerfully determined is God's plan for worship in our church, even if it's not my first choice?

As we yield to God's rule, we demonstrate we are truly worshipping Him with our entire being and life.

Chapter 12

BE STILL

I am a Type-A personality. I am energized by taking on a challenge, being proactive rather than reactive in my work and life, keeping active, and generally being in motion. Don't get me wrong; there is nothing wrong with healthy activity and hard work, but sometimes even good activities can get out of balance, and we start spinning our wheels and wearing down the spiritual bearings that keep us intact. It's hard for me to throttle down and move a little more slowly, much less be still in my time with God each day. Sometimes I chase through my day so fast I don't even realize I'm moving at breakneck speed. To compound matters, I'm also a person who has flurries of ideas and a somewhat short attention span. When I'm getting out of bed in the morning, my thoughts start racing even before my feet hit the floor. There is a temptation to charge ahead into the day without some stillness-time with God in prayer and worship.

Still Time

I have learned from experience the absolute necessity of starting and ending my day with God. As a pastor and worship leader, I have also known the importance of spending a few minutes in prayer and quiet time before each service to allow God to "still and fill" my heart so I minister in His power and not my own.

To compound matters further, our culture barrages us with messages and devices that promise to make life easier but really end up demanding more of our attention and time, even creating more internal stress. Our logical solution is to multi-task, to cram in as much as quickly as we can and think three steps ahead of where we are right now. If you don't believe me, just think about how much time you spend on your smart phone, Facebook, Twitter, Internet, TV, or other media while you're trying to do something else.

With our multi-tasking lives, we end up living in the future, while we're in the present, in an attempt not to repeat the past. The real tragedy of this is that we miss some great moments God wants to give to us as a special gift, and instead, we end up with more stress-related conditions, thoughts, and lives. So right now, let's put the brakes on for a couple of minutes and consider God's path to peace and balance in life. Listen to what God says:

Be still, and know that I am God; I will be exalted among the nations, I will be exalted in the earth. (Ps. 46:10)

Psalm 46 is both a compassionate promise by God and a stern warning. To those who quietly trust God for shelter and care, God tells us to "Be calm and rest in the knowledge that I am your God, who will now and always be with you" (my wording). This psalm is also a somber and stern command from God to people who clamor for control and push their own agendas over God's plan. God's word is this: "Be quiet! Enough with your noise! I am God, and I alone am in control and will have the final word and glory in all things" (again, my wording).

Being still before God is not an option. The reality is that either by our choice to worship Him or by God's command, someday all will stand silently before God.

So much of "being still" before God is letting go of the control we consciously or unconsciously seek in our lives and circumstances. Often we can't see our need to be in charge of our circumstances until we turn off the internal motor of our life to simply be with God. A *huge* part of surrendering in worship involves trusting God to take care of the things that concern us while we are in His presence, especially the things that seem out of control in our lives. For many of us, this is a huge risk. It means facing and releasing our fear of being "not in control" to God and then resting in Him for the answers and outcomes.

This kind of worshipful stillness and trust leads followers of Jesus to "seek first the kingdom of God and His righteousness," knowing that "all these things will be given to you as well" (Matt. 6:33). God will take care of our concerns when we first concern ourselves with Him. Jesus went off alone to be with the Father on a regular basis, and His to-do list was a *lot* bigger than ours. Quiet time with God was a lifestyle practice of Jesus that extended all the way to Gethsemane the night before His death on the cross. If Jesus needed this time with God, how much more do we?

Wait and Listen

Are you unsure if you can do it? Well, ask God to empower you and then just try this out for the next fourteen days and see what happens:

- Carve out ten to fifteen minutes each day of "still" time with God. Note: you may need to wake up before the kids in order to do this. It's worth it.
- Turn off any distracting or unnecessary noise.
- Start by taking a couple of minutes to decompress by emptying outside thoughts, worries, and personal battles to God. It's okay. He told us to cast our cares on Him. This can be either a verbal or, better yet, written outpouring of your thoughts.
- Next, ask God to still your mind and heart. Begin by breathing a little more slowly, and pray, "Speak, Lord, your servant is listening" (1 Sam. 3:10).

Finally, wait and listen for God. Let His Word silently fill you. God may direct you to read and reflect on a scripture that comes to mind. Read I Kings 19:11–12. God spoke to Elijah in a still, small voice. Here are a couple quieting scriptures to help you get started:

The Lord will fight for you; you need only to be still. (Ex. 14:14)

Be still before the Lord and wait patiently for him; do not fret when people succeed in their ways, when they carry out their wicked schemes. (Ps. 37:7)

My heart is not proud, Lord, my eyes are not haughty; I do not concern myself with great matters or things too wonderful for me. But I have calmed and quieted myself, I am like a weaned child with its mother; like a weaned child I am content. Israel, put your hope in the Lord both now and forevermore. (Ps. 131)

As a songwriter, I know that good music is comprised of sounds and spaces of silence called rests. The word *selah* that appears in many of the psalms was actually an instruction for God's people during worship. Many scholars hold that selah moments in Old Testament worship were times for God's people to be still and reflect on what they had just heard or sung in a psalm.

Selah moments are good for us in our times of personal worship. We become still before God and revel in Who He is and all He has done for us.

Worship, like music, isn't complete until there are spaces of silence between the sounds and activities in our life and time with God.

Chapter 13
SEARCH

I f you've ever been to the doctor for a physical examination, or undergone tests to check on a health concern, you know that personal vanity and pride need to get checked at the door. The doctor inspects, pokes, prods, and sees things that we probably wish no one would ever see. Our need to know what is going on and get it healed, fixed, or removed is greater than our desire to let people see only what we want them to see: the best parts of us. We are willing to submit to the doctor because we trust that he or she wants the best for us and can hopefully do something to help us live longer and healthier lives. Isaiah humbly met the Divine, the Great Physician, who diagnosed his spiritual sickness and then delivered the cure to him in the form of a hot coal.

At some point, as we continue to surrender ourselves to God in worship, we will be led to echo the words of the psalmist:

> Search me, O God, and know my heart, test me and know my anxious thoughts, see if there is any offensive way in me and lead me in the way everlasting. (Ps.139:23–24)

Confession

One misunderstood part of worship is the practice of confession. Some of us have memories of confession as a religious act that may or may not have been authentic or even healthy. Others think of confession in terms of magazines or TV shows that "expose" the real-life dark sides of celebrities, with no sense of boundaries, personal concern, truth, or desire for life change. The unfortunate side effect of this is that many people have thrown out confession to God as an outdated, archaic, or unhealthy thing, something to be avoided at all costs.

Others run from confession because it's easier to bury our junk in the backyard of our souls, unaware of the pollution it is creating in our spirit.

The reality of heartfelt confession in worship, however, is that it comes out of an authentic, desperate trust in God and His unfailing love for us. Real confession happens when our need to come clean with God (and people we have hurt) is greater than our natural tendencies to put on a false front and hide what is going on inside us. Our relationship with God matters more than our reputation or image.

The Depth of God's Love

It is only when we fall backwards into the arms of God's mercy and love that we will know the depth of His love for us. That is both the irony and beauty of confession. Psalm 139 beautifully displays the writer's awareness of God's presence in his life, from his mother's womb to the present. He also acknowledges that God *already* knows everything about him, so there is no hiding from Him. Implied in this psalm is the writer's confidence and declaration that God alone is able to abolish evil, both in each person and in the world. Finally, the psalmist gives God, the Divine Physician, permission to do a spiritual examination of every facet of his life and being. Take a moment and ask God to do the same for you as you reflect on these verses from Psalm 139:

"Search me, O God, and know my heart": Lord, please check my spiritual foundation, my motives, my hopes, my dreams, my desires, and my integrity.

"Test me and know my anxious thoughts": God, please examine the cares, worries, and issues that weigh me down and keep me from walking in faith.

"See if there is any offensive way in me": God, I give you permission to look at the blind spots and dark regions in me that are ugly and repulsive. I submit to your divine searchlight to shed light on sinful attitudes, thoughts, and behaviors in me.

"Lead me in the way everlasting": My Savior and God, change me from the inside out so I may experience spiritual health and eternal life in You, beginning right now.

As you pray this psalm, be mindful of what God may be revealing to you. It may be a person you have hurt, a sinful act, an attitude or a bad habit that He is asking you to bring forward. Like going to the doctor, we need to submit both to God's examination and His prescription for our life. The submission to God's prescription is what we call "repentance." It's not earning God's forgiveness, but following His lead when He tells us to go and sin no more.

In this process of confession, it is important to let God's grace and forgiveness wash over you like a flood, and then determine, by His power, that this sin is history and God is now your director and controller, so this will never happen again. Then obediently go and take care of the spiritual "clean up" that God leads you to do to seal the deal. The sign of real forgiveness is your personal willingness to submit to God and bring reconciliation to others as well. Once this is done, it is *done*, so don't keep revisiting the same issue over and over. Instead, thank God for His forgiveness that was bought for you by Jesus's blood on the cross. It is time for all followers of Jesus Christ to reclaim the healthy act of worship that is found in authentic, transparent confession and repentance.

Chapter 14

AGREEMENTS

People sometimes live their lives based on assumptions and things they've been taught or told are true—when in fact they are wrong. Here are a few examples:

- "The earth is the center of the universe."
- "People will never make a machine that can fly like a bird."
- "God could never accept me because of what I've done."

False Agreements

Wrongly held beliefs, like these, create in people what some have called false agreements. When we adopt these beliefs in our life, we make conscious and subconscious agreements that cause us to build our thoughts and behavior on what turns out to be a house of cards. Even more tragically, when we live our lives based on false agreements, we miss out on exciting opportunities to grow and go with God in ways beyond our misguided thinking. For a moment, Isaiah thought he was going to receive the death penalty from God because he was "a man of unclean lips who lived among a people of unclean lips." Don't get me wrong; Isaiah and the people he lived among were full of sin. Even if only for a moment, Isaiah wrongly bought into the idea that God was more focused on judging and destroying him than in saving him. His subsequent experience with God showed him that even as God judges in righteousness, He also loves, forgives, and cleanses people who say yes to Him.

Recently my nephew Jesse was selected to be a contestant on the television program *The Biggest Loser*. Jesse began the program at a weight of 367 pounds, but by the time the show was over, he weighed 201 pounds, a loss of 166 pounds. How did he accomplish this? First, Jesse entered this show realizing that his life was at stake. He was willing to be humbled by nationally broadcasted weigh-ins; grueling workouts that break people to tears and exhaustion; and gut-wrenching sessions with trainers, doctors, and a dietician. Jesse was also willing to look deep inside at the false agreements he had made with food throughout his life. Jesse had to be confronted with the fact that his excess body weight was symptomatic of a deeper problem: accepting as reality things that were not true or healthy. These false overlays warped his sense of worth and purpose and had to be confronted and corrected in order for him to lose weight for a TV program and keep the weight off for the rest of his life. Today, Jesse continues to maintain a healthy body weight and is helping other people lose weight and develop healthy lifestyles.

At times, *all* of us, including those who have followed Jesus Christ for years or even decades, need to be confronted with the fact that we have heard and accepted things that are actually artificial, destructive falsehoods that have no basis in God's Word. Like Jesse, we need to come to grips with the fact that our very spiritual health is at stake. False agreements pull us away from God and His plan for us, yet we hold onto them for dear life, even as they poison us spiritually. It's important we don't easily dismiss ourselves from looking inside because we think we're above this issue. The reality is that we *all* have made false agreements and God wants to set us free so we can live in the new freedom He bought for each of us on the cross.

It is for freedom that Christ has set us free. Stand firm, then, and do not let yourselves be burdened again by a yoke of slavery. (Gal. 5:1)

Apart from those truths that directly flow from God's Word, I am convinced many things we have held as true will be revealed to us in heaven as being false, human-made constructs. These are the things we need to surrender to God as we ask and allow Him to transform us in worship. These false constructs can come in many forms and from many sources, including the following:

- Legalistic traditions, worship forms, styles of music (both traditional and modern)
- Non-biblical philosophies falsely superimposed onto God's Word
- Past spiritual, emotional, or physical abuse that creates lies about the victim's self-worth as well as his or her perceptions of worth in God's eyes
- Self-centered, destructive beliefs, patterns, and lifestyles conveyed by film, TV, movies, print media, and spokespeople of the toxic culture in which we live

New Agreements

The first step is to ask God to open your eyes to see your false agreements. God's desire is for you to be free of these chains. This freedom starts with a new agreement, one that agrees with God's Word that simply but powerfully states truth:

If the Son sets you free, you are free indeed. (John 8:36)

FREEDOM

Read Luke 8:1–2.

The people in the area where Mary the Magdalene lived thought they knew who she was, evil spirits and all. Mary bought into that agreement as well. Then she encountered Jesus Christ, who freed her from the spiritual bondage that enslaved her and shattered the false agreements within her. Because of Jesus, Mary realized she was now a called and chosen daughter of the most-high God. Her place in the Bible is well documented. She stayed close to Jesus at the cross and was one of the first to see the risen Christ on Easter morning.

The lesson: Jesus has power to free us from what enslaves us and break the false agreements we have made. Most important, He is always with us!

Even as Christ has set us free, it is *very* important that God gives us the fellowship and gifts of other believers to help us learn, grow, and live in that freedom. Just as Jesse sought help from gifted trainers, followers of Christ also need to seek help in finding God's perspectives, teaching, and support from a spiritually healthy church—not just any church, but one that both preaches and practices grace and growth in God and His Word. Once you've found a church to attend, don't remain anonymous and alone. Join a Bible study, worship regularly, listen to insightful,

Word-based teaching, work with a trained pastoral counselor, and meet with other committed Christ-followers for support and accountability. With God's help and the support of other Christ-followers, you can experience and enjoy the freedom of seeing old, false agreements die and new, God-filled agreements become the growing reality in your life.

Stepping into the new agreements with God, yourself, and others is an important act of worship and submission to God. Don't be surprised if one day you find yourself, like Jesse, helping others to experience the freedom you have found.

Chapter 15

GETTING OUT, LETTING IN

S ometimes worship can be painful. Isaiah had to admit to God, in the midst of heavenly perfection, that he was full of sin and was unclean.

I'm not talking about pain caused by self-mutilation or destructive behavior. I'm also not speaking about a pain we inflict on ourselves in order to clear up or pay our way out of guilt. That's what the Bible calls self-justification, and it is literally a dead-end street of failure and eternal emptiness.

Rather, I'm pointing to a pain that leads to healing: our admission (to the one and only God, to whom we've given our heart and life, and possibly also to another person who loves and trusts us) that we have failed to live the way we were redeemed and called to live. This is the very definition of sin. More often than we realize, each and every one of us needs to fess up to God (and probably to another person) that we have thought, said, or done something wrong. We have slandered God and hurt others and ourselves by our callous and ungodly behavior.

Confession is admitting that, although we are made in God's image and purchased by Jesus into God's forever family, we've screwed up and need to come clean before God so we can again walk with Him in forgiveness, grace, healing, and freedom. Confession is also the starting point of the painful but worthwhile journey to restore relationships with God's other family members.

It will likely be humiliating, embarrassing, and yes, even painful to do this. But confession is the only road to experiencing God's love, grace, healing, and power in a profound and life-altering way.

We are often deceived into thinking it's better to keep our sins inside. Consider the expression: "What they don't know won't hurt them." Or maybe, "Just don't think about it, and it will be okay."

Wrong. Things kept buried inside the inner chambers of our mind, like old bones, will surface again—often during personal storms or other unexpected moments. And in the meantime, the buried trash of our sin poisons our spiritual life—and even our emotional and physical being. The old gardening axiom holds true to confession: it's better to pull weeds when they first appear than to wait until they're full-grown and overrunning the garden.

Getting Out

Psalm 51 is David's "getting it out" confession song. Here is the larger-than-life giant-slayer, man-after-God's-own-heart, King of Israel admitting heinous sins of adultery and murder. David's confession came as the direct result of the loving and truth-telling prophet Nathan. He strategically helped David realize the magnitude of what he had done against God and other people. The result? David was broken by this painful truth-session. He immediately left behind his stealth strategy of hiding sin and moved into the open-air approach to getting it out into the light of God's truth.

David had to admit to God that he had sinned. This was painful. He had to leave behind his desire to look good in front of all of Israel. This was also painful. He had to endure the consequences of what he had done. This was very painful.

Yet he did it. Why?

Because at the core of his being, David really loved God and wanted more than anything to have a restored, forever relationship with God.

God is always open-armed, and He loves people who confess their sins with hearts that desperately long for a changed life and a right relationship with Him and those they have wronged.

In our confession there needs to be a commitment in the deepest part of our being that says, "By God's grace, I'm never going down that road again." Confession is not about brushing off an offense we have done as small or inconsequential. It is never about taking the easy way out. It is *always* about getting out what the enemy and our own pride would tempt us to keep locked inside.

At times our worship needs to be filled with the tears of confessing that our lives are broken and in need of the fresh air of forgiveness and restoration. It is a painful thing that leads to the sweet, rarified air of God's grace.

Letting In

Worship inherently involves surrendering to God, and surrendering involves both "getting out" and "letting in."

Equally important to "getting out" our mistakes, flaws, and sins through confession is the process of letting in God's forgiveness and grace.

The underlying motive for authentic confession is a deep, personal brokenness and remorse that we have hurt God and others. Real confession can only happen when we realize in the deepest part of our being that we cannot keep hiding or justifying what we have done. Our very spiritual core aches until we get *all* our sinful garbage out in the open, because God sees it anyway. In confession, we throw ourselves at God's divine mercy in an act of profound and even painful admission of who we are and what we have done. Confession is not given with the intention of going back and repeating our past mistakes. It is the first step in a process of allowing God to reorder and re-establish our life and relationship with Him and other people.

However, the dark reality of confession—without reception of God's grace and forgiveness—is that it can become a futile exercise in self-justification. Confession without letting God do whatever He wants to do in us is really false-idol self-worship. Why? Because we are still in control, and God is only there at our beck and call to do the forgiving so we can continue to be in control. Without receiving God's grace and power, there is no real internal change. Instead, it's all about "feeling better" so that we can get back to the life we're used to.

I saw a TV program a couple of months ago in which a young man was asked why he went through the exercise of confession at his church every week. He simply stated that he liked doing whatever he wanted every other day and confession each Saturday was his way of feeling better so he could keep up his same lifestyle and behavior. I wanted to reach into our TV and plead with him that what he thought was confession was nothing more than a self-centered, self-righteous act to soothe the guilt that was obviously ravaging him inside.

Make no mistake about it; God hates sin. God also loves to forgive people.

Jesus readily forgave the worst of sinners: the woman caught in the act of adultery, a tax man who cheated people out of their hard-earned money, and many others. But also take note that none of these people offered a self-defense, excuse, or rationale for themselves or their behavior. Jesus knew the profound brokenness in them because he saw their hearts, and He offered them deep forgiveness and grace, a kind they had never experienced before.

But when Jesus told them they were forgiven, he also said, "Follow me," and "Go, and sin no more" (John 8:11). He pointed them to a new road to walk on, rather than giving them permission to go back to the old ways of their broken lives. And you know what? These people did exactly what Jesus asked, because they experienced His love and power. They were profoundly changed because they let Him in.

We need to get out the sin that ravages us inside. Next, we need to let God in as we come to Him in worship:

- Letting in really means letting God into the darkest corners of our minds and hearts, both past and present. We have to let God's searing, loving light into our very being so He can kill the rotting spiritual mold of our sin.
- Letting in involves letting God not only cleanse us, but also transform us. Whether the first time or the ten-thousandth time, God is continuously at work to change us into the masterpiece He created us to be, moving us from glory to glory.
- Letting in also means letting Him take charge of our future by saying, "I will go where you call me to go, and I will never go

back to where I've been. I will do this not by my power, but by your grace and power you've placed in me."

Finally, letting in means we need to truly receive what God says about our sins. Once confessed and forgiven, He has put them away from us, "as far away as East is from the West" (Ps. 103). Trace your finger around a globe, and you'll quickly see that when you move to the east at no point do you ever start traveling west, or vice-versa. In other words, in terms of our spiritual destiny, our sins will never meet us again in God's eyes, even if we need to live the consequences of our actions while still on earth.

So, confess to God—and to those He prompts you to go to—the secret sins that have been buried deep within you. Then receive, truly *receive*, the gift of God's forgiveness and restored relationship. Finally, don't dwell on past sins confessed and forgiven. Instead, thank God and celebrate that you are in a new position with Him, free and forgiven.

—— Reflections on Surrendering to God in Worship ——

As we open ourselves to God, we realize He loves us deeply.

Perspectives

What are your first-thought perspectives and reflections on surrendering to God in worship? What strikes you as important, interesting, or challenging?

Foundations

Acknowledgment, trust, and humility are at the heart of "yielding and surrendering" to God. What does that mean to you? What changes would that mean for you?

God says He opposes the proud, but gives grace to the humble (James 4:6). Why is humility so important in worship?

Insights

God wants to touch us, change us, and bring us to a better place through worship. God asks us to willingly and continually surrender ourselves to Him and to His forgiveness, power, and grace. Even as we yield to God, we recognize that healing and grace come only from God's hand, not by our efforts.

Yielding and obedience allow God's grace and healing to enter in. How can you integrate this into living in this world? What are some steps you might take to yield and obey daily?

Confession, forgiveness, and God's saving grace: How do you embrace these? What falsehoods and obstacles need to be cleared away for you to do so?

Be still and listen to God. What is God saying to you now?

Application

How do you see Part 3's "Surrendering" insights as challenging, changing, or reinforcing your perspectives and experience? How are you being called closer to God in worship?

How might you apply this?

PART 4

EXPERIENCING GOD

The essence of worship is to experience God and be changed.

This occurs both in our personal time with God and when we gather with others in God-directed and empowered worship.

When we experience God, we are filled with the energy and desire to live more and more for Him.

Chapter 16

THIRSTY AND HUNGRY

Thirsty

We're all thirsty people. I'm not talking just about our need for water to keep our bodies hydrated. Inside each of us is a deep soul-thirst for something greater than ourselves, something divine.

I am a runner and know from a painful month of kidney stones a few years ago that keeping hydrated is essential to good health. After these stones were blasted away, my doctor informed me it was a lack of sufficient water in my system that caused calcified stones to form in my kidneys. Interestingly, in those days, I was attracted to sugary, caffeinated drinks like soda to "quench" my thirst, when in fact those were the very things that were taking away needed water from my body. What I really needed was pure water.

It's like that with the spiritual thirst we all experience. We are drawn to the quick-fix, easy ways of trying to quench the soul-need in us, only to find out they not only don't satisfy us in the long run, but they also exact a damaging toll on us and the lives of other people. This has been the story of humanity for generations. Read what God spoke to the Israelites through the prophet Jeremiah:

My people have committed two sins: They have forsaken me, the spring of living water, and have dug their own cisterns, broken cisterns that cannot hold water. (Jer. 2:13)

We all try to take care of our own soul-thirst, but ultimately find that our so-called solutions don't hold water. Chances are, many of us never even gave a second thought to God when we starting digging our own wells.

Do any of these self-made wells sound familiar?

- Turning to alcohol or drugs to fill the void of our emptiness
- Using other people through sex to get a short-term high
- Measuring our self-worth by career success or expensive things
- Looking for the next relationship that will hopefully make me feel like I'm somebody
- Self-mutilating by excessive eating, cutting, or other destructive behaviors
- Getting lost in video worlds and online surreal activity
- Doing busy things—even church activity—to mask the unhappiness or emptiness we feel inside
- Putting pressure on our kids to achieve so we can live vicariously through them and finally feel successful

This is just a starter list to which I'm sure you could add your own story. After reflecting on your life so far, take a few minutes to honestly evaluate your spiritual thirst. Where do you put yourself on this continuum?

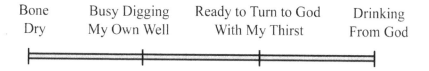

| Bone Dry | Busy Digging My Own Well | Ready to Turn to God With My Thirst | Drinking From God |

Wherever you are now, your thirst and hunger for meaning in life can still be satisfied, even if you're bone dry or tired of digging your own well of fulfillment. As long as you can still fog a mirror, it's not too late to turn to God and experience the eternal water that He alone can provide to fill your soul. Worship is the ongoing process of turning away from our own empty wells and turning to God for the fulfillment of the deepest hunger and thirst of our life.

Taste and See

My wife and I are big fans of food-related television programs, especially competitive cooking shows. There is one program in particular we watch whenever possible. It's a show in which four accomplished chefs face off with each other in a limited time period to prepare meals from a mystery basket of foods. A panel of three celebrity chefs critique each course of the three-part meal. At the end of each course, the panel votes off ("chops") one chef from the competition until only one remains. That person is awarded a substantial cash prize and earns the title "champion." We've learned a lot about unique ingredients and cooking techniques from watching this show, and we really enjoy the vivid descriptions of the chef-prepared meals and flavors that the host and judges experience. But there's one *big* difference between the judges' experience and ours. They can taste the prepared food. We can't.

There's nothing like actually tasting what we see. Most chefs will tell you we eat first with our eyes. But the experience would be less than satisfying if it ended there. We must also taste and experience the goodness of the food we eat.

Our experience of worshipping God can be just like watching a TV show about food. If we are only spectators in worshipping God, we will see what worship looks like, but we will miss the key ingredient: tasting God. Read what Psalm 34:8 states: "Taste and see that the LORD is good."

The meaning of this verse is not merely to admire God from a distance, but to personally experience Him in all His goodness. The essence of worship, as Isaiah discovered, was not the "wow factor" of the watching and hearing the mighty angels in their worship of God, as awesome as that must have been. That was only the prelude to the main event: encountering God face to face. Isaiah's tasting of God's goodness made all the difference and forever changed the path of his life.

It's beyond my comprehension why God, who is the very definition of holiness and greatness, would want us to taste His goodness. But He does. God's love for us goes so far beyond our human understanding that He invites and even desires to have us experience Him fully, regardless of our past and failures. Jesus encourages us to go in and climb right up on Abba's lap, since we're now adopted, fully vested, and loved daughters and sons of the Most High God. More than anything else, our Heavenly Father wants to be with us, His children. Encountering God in worship is so much more than taking in the external trappings, including what we see, smell, or feel in any worship experience. The God-designed purpose of worship is that we experience Him personally.

I invite you to try something for the next twenty-one days. First, read both scripture verses below, then read them out loud. There is something very powerful about speaking God's Word with your voice in addition to thinking about it. Each day, personalize each of these verses by inserting your name where I've indicated, and then spend a few minutes asking and waiting on God to show you how to experience Him even more fully.

With joy [say your name here] will draw water from the wells of salvation. (Is. 12:3)

Taste and see that the LORD is good; blessed is [again, speak your name here] who takes refuge in him. (Ps. 34:8)

Do this every day for three weeks and watch how God satisfies the deepest thirst and desire He has placed in you. You'll discover the ultimate worship encounter begins when we say *yes* to God's invitation to taste and see how good He really is.

Chapter 17

THE NEW FOUNTAIN

esus met a woman at a well in the region called Samaria. I imagine
she looked a lot like some women I have seen, whose faces show the
hardness and deep wrinkles of years of cigarette smoking, gambling
addiction, hard drinking, and relationship hopping. In human terms,
this Samaritan woman had three strikes against her. First, she was part
Jewish and part pagan; thus, she was considered less than human to many
of the Jews of her day. Second, she was also a woman and, therefore, not
valued as much as a male in her culture. Finally, she had been married
and divorced five times. So, she was far outside the boundary lines of
morality in the eyes of most religious people of her time. The holes of
her self-dug wells littered her life, and the results were plain to see. She
probably came in the heat of the day, well after the time respectable
people would go there to get their daily jugs of water.

It was exactly at this time that Jesus approached her at the well
in a small town called Sychar. He first asked her for a drink, knowing

full well that it was a social no-no for a Jewish man (especially a rabbi) to even associate with an immoral, Samaritan woman. Jesus didn't care about that. His purpose was to offer her something that would change her forever.

Living Water

During the course of their conversation, Jesus offered her something he called "living water" that would cause her never to thirst again. This was a new kind of spiritual water that would quench the deepest need in a person and become a kind of life-giving internal spring, welling up inside that person all the way into eternity. In other words, this new water would not only fill her emptiness, but would also pour out through her into other people's lives.

She was curious, but didn't understand what in the world he was talking about. So Jesus took the unusual but deeply personal step of revealing he knew all about her and the empty wells that had haunted her all her life: the failed relationships and the outcast-ness of her life. He *knew* she was thirsty and was offering her a new start and a never-ending source of spiritual fulfillment.

When she pointed out the differences between Jewish and Samaritan worship, Jesus gave her a new definition of real worship, one that has nothing to do with the religious externals she was focused on. Here's what He told her:

An hour is coming, and now is, when the true worshippers will worship the Father in spirit and truth, for such people the Father seeks to be His worshippers. God is spirit, and those who worship Him must worship in spirit and in truth. (John 4:23–24, NASB)

Still not understanding what Jesus meant, the woman told Him she knew that the Messiah, when He comes, would explain everything. Jesus then told her He *is* the Messiah.

And then the light bulb came on in her heart and mind. Jesus had just explained everything to her. He really *is* the Messiah, the promised Savior!

Life-Changing Awareness

The woman had a life-changing realization and decision. Just like Isaiah, she had encountered God Himself, the God who sought and came to *her*, who showed her He knows her and loves her. Most important, in Jesus the Messiah the woman came to know and experience God alone can satisfy the deepest need and thirst of her life. This Samaritan woman personally encountered God, who came to her despite her past, failures, and social-outcast standing.

As with Isaiah, the trajectory of her life dramatically changed. The Samaritan came away a new woman who impacted other people in her hometown with her spirit-filled, truthful telling of who Jesus is and what He did for her. Interestingly, the biblical account states she even left her old water jar behind at the well, implying the new well inside her was freely flowing.

Authentic worship is all about coming to God "just as I am, without one plea" and allowing Him to pour Himself into us: heart, mind, soul, and being. At its heart, worship is also about the new relationship God wants with each of us. The amazing miracle Jesus revealed to this woman is that God desires to pour Himself into anyone who will say yes to Him. Think about it: no one can ever worship God "in the Spirit and in truth" (John 4:23) unless God Himself implants His Spirit like a well inside us, and unless He imparts His Truth like a fountain in us.

God has initiated this new relationship and wants to meet with you at the well today and every day, so that in His spirit and truth, a never-ending source of His power, love, and grace will fill up in you and flow out into others.

Chapter 18

GOD-DIRECTED WORSHIP

The difference between rote, lifeless worship activities and a dynamic encounter with God in worship involves choosing between two diametrically different approaches in our personal and corporate worship times. We can choose to be self-conscious or self-less in our worship. Either choice has consequences.

The Self-Conscious Approach

We can totally miss God because we are unwilling to risk embarrassment or a "PR hit" to our dignity if we partake in an unashamed, real expression of worship to God. The reward of the self-conscious approach is that we offend no one—except God. The truth is we sometimes fear being misunderstood or criticized by people more than we fear God when we give him a people-tainted, half-baked, half-hearted worship offering.

The God-Conscious Approach

This is the "go-for-it" way, with real praise, exuberance, tears, mourning, confession, and heartfelt worship to God. This approach stretches us beyond our comfort zone, upbringing, and culture. The reward is simply experiencing God's presence, power, and grace more than even words can express. It can also bring criticism from people. There are many examples of people in the Bible who chose worshipping God over what other people might think of or even do to them. Let's look at just one of them today, David.

David, the musician-shepherd, Goliath-slayer, and King of Israel, rejoiced when the ark of God, long missing from Jerusalem, was finally found and returned to the city. After he sacrificed an offering to God, we are told he joyfully danced with all his might before the Lord while a vast throng from Israel blared victorious trumpets and raised shouts of happiness as they brought the ark into Jerusalem.

David led the entire nation of Israel in a selfless and spontaneous display of thanks, praise, and worship to God, even inadvertently losing some of his clothing in the process. This exuberant display would be akin to having the President of the United States so thrilled that the national debt was finally, miraculously erased (one can still hope) that he led the whole country in a victory dance down the streets of Washington, D.C.

You would think everyone would have approved of this, and you would be wrong. David's own wife, Michal, is described as seeing King David "leaping and dancing before the Lord," and she consequently despised him (see 2 Sam 6:20–23). She even accused David of disrobing in front of people like a vulgar person. Michal was only concerned about David's corporate image, the way a king ought to behave, not his relationship with God. David's response to her revealed that his heart first and foremost belonged to God. He told her, "I will celebrate before the Lord. I will become even more undignified than this, and I will be humiliated in my own eyes." David's first priority was worshipping God, rather than doing anything for the approval of people.

Michal tellingly disappears from the pages of Scripture after this exchange with David, with the postscript that she "had no children to the day of her death." David, on the other hand, was used by God as Israel's king and the ancestor of Jesus.

We all come from different cultural backgrounds. Perhaps you, like me, came from an upbringing in which you were taught to keep expressions of emotion and worship inside and subdued. The challenge for all of us is to let the reality of what God is doing inside be shown on the outside—regardless of our upbringing or what people may or may not think of us. Many of the people I know who caution against dynamic singing, arm-raising, or tears during worship are the same ones who stand, cheer, or well up when their favorite team finally wins the championship. It seems to me the Champion of all champions—Jesus Christ—deserves all this passion and more.

Fragrant Worship

What does worship smell like? Mary, the sister of Lazarus and Martha, teaches us a lot about what makes worship fragrant to God. To set the scene, chapter 12 of John's Gospel recounts how Jesus, shortly after raising Lazarus from the dead, was sitting at a dinner table in the home of Lazarus, Mary, and Martha, three grown siblings and friends of Jesus. Imagine the sense of Mary's exuberance and wonder to see her brother "Laz" breathing, eating, laughing, and talking after three days dead in the tomb. This had to be almost surreal. What profound awe and gratitude Mary must have felt when she realized Jesus brought Lazarus back from the dead. That experience was enough to convince her Jesus was who He said He was: God's Son, The Messiah! She desperately wanted to express the fullness in her heart at that moment.

But what could she give him as an act of worship and thanks for what he had done for her? It had to be both an extravagant and meaningful gift. Perhaps she saw the blisters on Jesus's feet or the dry, cracked skin that must have been so painful for him. Then it came to her. Mary gathered what some say was equivalent to one year's salary and bought a pint of nard to soothe the tired and sore feet of this man she now knew was the Messiah, the Christ. Mary broke open the expensive, perfumed oil and began pouring it over Jesus's feet. The biblical account states "the house was filled with the fragrance of the perfume" (John 12:1). She even used her hair to wipe off the excess, acting just like a servant in tending to the master. It was a heartfelt and real act of worship that Mary put her whole self, including her hair, into doing!

Then the opposition sparks flew. Judas was livid when he saw her action and called her out in front of everyone. He derided her, saying the money she spent to buy the nard could have been used to help poor people, which is ironic given the fact that he had his own hand in the till. It's interesting that the same, sweet perfume Jesus smelled was offensive to Judas, who was about to betray Him.

So what was God's response to this event? Jesus rose to the woman's defense and let everyone know her action was not only beautiful but also had significance with His approaching death and burial, something the disciples would only understand after the cross and resurrection. In Mark's Gospel account, Jesus told us the woman's extravagant act of worship would be told in memory of her (Mark 14:8), which is what we are doing right now.

It's Time for a Heart Check

- Are you ever moved to give God an extravagant act of worship out of love for Him? Have you ever boldly done this?
- Do other people's acts of worship cause you to feel embarrassment, bitterness, or anger? What do you think is the underlying cause of these feelings?
- What is keeping you from "pouring out your heart to God" in worship?

A full year's salary. This was a lavish demonstration of faith from a woman of limited financial means. What is God asking you to do in faith to bless Him and others for His kingdom's sake?

Your worship offering may or may not be expensive, but it is always costly in that we put ourselves out there when we express our heartfelt worship to Him, both privately and in worship with other believers. Worship that smells sweet to God is that which flows out of a deep sense of awe and love for Him. I invite you to take your eyes off of other people and keep your heart and worship directed at God alone. Worship Him with all your heart and might!

Chapter 19

CONDUIT AND FUEL

Conduit

I once served as a worship consultant for a church that had built a new worship center just prior to my coming. As I began to work in the worship center, it became apparent there were some serious problems with the sound system, which would require major repairs and improvements. Some of the repairs required new wiring to be installed. When we investigated running new cables from the amp room to the sound board and platform, we discovered that half of the in-floor conduit lines intended for running cables to and from different areas were unusable because they had been crushed by the weight of the concrete poured over them during the construction.

This image leads me to my point. Like it or not, we are a conduit for something in life. We can be a conduit for God's divine blessing, hope, faith, and love, as He created us to be, or we can be a conduit of pessimism, selfishness, turmoil, bitterness, and a host of other things that run amuck of God's plan for us and other people.

Let me be perfectly clear. What runs in and through the conduit is what matters, not the conduit itself. But when the weight of life's circumstances or our own poor attitudes and choices distorts or even blocks the conduit that God intends for us to be, then we need to look at repairing, rebuilding, and protecting the conduit. We do this so that what moves in and through us—God's Holy Spirit—can do so freely and unencumbered by obstacles or barriers of our making or by pressures from the world outside.

How do we strengthen and protect the conduit of our life so that God's Spirit will continue to move in and through us? I would suggest we allow God to retrain the way we look at and react to life, intentionally deciding to become people of praise. This is not just a decision to voice some meaningless words. It is really a matter of training our hearts to acknowledge and see God moving in and above all things.

The word *praise* may cause some of us to squirm a little, as we may have associated it with the caricature of a weird (and sometimes phony) religious fanatic who seemed more about outward appearance than the inner reality of God's grace in his or her life. But praise is so much more than a simple religious expression. In fact, the dictionary defines praise as the act of expressing admiration and gratefulness for a benefit or favor.

A few years ago, I had a memorable encounter with Dave Riebe, a painter whose work I admired for many years. It was by unusual and serendipitous circumstances that my family and I happened to meet him at an art show in Grand Marais, Minnesota. When I realized who he was, I couldn't help but pour out my heart and let him know how his paintings inspired me. The experience of meeting him brought about heartfelt expressions of joy and appreciation. Believe me, it was rich praise I gave to him. As I reflected on this later, I realized I felt richer for telling him. I actually benefited from giving him praise for his work.

This is an illustration of what praise can look like in our worship life with God. A big part of worshipping God is pouring out what is inside us to Him. Praise also teaches us to remember and call to mind all the good things God has done in us and for us. I am convinced that when we do this, we come away spiritually richer and alive—even more joyful.

My desire is to dedicate more of my worship time to letting God know how much He means to me, even when life isn't understandable or easy. The challenge is that I often get caught in the "here's my problem" approach to prayer. Even as God tells us to cast our worries and cares on Him, there is a hidden danger that we will focus more on our problems than on God, who can do infinitely more than we could ever ask for or imagine. Praise takes the focus off the problem and onto the eternal, everlasting Problem Solver.

Becoming a conduit of praise to God begins with a choice each day to express our admiration and love to God, as well as a deep appreciation for what He has done for us. I invite you to join me in choosing to develop a new heart habit of praise, for all God is, for all He is to you, for all He has done, for all He has done for you, for all He is doing, for all He is doing in you, and for all that is to come.

When we allow ourselves to consider all of this, we will experience God and know in the depth of our being that He is worth every ounce of our praise—and much more.

Fuel

Several years ago, I bought a portable, gas-powered electric generator from my brother-in-law. It was a brand-new, year-end model that had never been used, and he offered to sell it to me at a price I couldn't refuse. I asked my wife and told her it would be great insurance against a power outage. I envisioned using it for outdoor concerts, power tools, and more. So we took the offer and bought it.

It then sat in my garage for several years. Yes, *years,* without once getting started. No fuel, no starting it up, and no test runs—just taking up space in our garage. Now, once it finally got started, it has since been used many times for church services and concerts, youth events, for a friend who needed it for her RV, and yes, even for some cool outdoor construction projects when regular electrical current was not available.

But the generator also taught me something about worship. Actually, the generator is a little like all of us when we worship God.

Don't get me wrong, I'm not saying we are merely machines that God manipulates and uses as He pleases. God loves each of us with an everlasting love. He put us in an amazing position of leadership and stewardship in all of His creation and gave us each a free will to choose to love Him or not, to follow Him or not. In that regard, we are much different from any machine.

But stay with me on this. Like a generator, each of us has the right pieces and mechanisms put in place to accomplish what we were built to do when we were created. God made us all, above any other creature on this planet, fully capable of worshipping, living for, and serving Him. He built us each with a specific purpose and plan, and He did so with loving care.

With a generator, unless the owner puts the right fuel in place, the generator is lifeless and can do nothing of value. Water won't work. Putting sugar in a gas tank will doom an engine. The generator needs the right gas and oil mixture in order to produce something of power the owner can use for his purposes.

As God-built generators, we need the right fuel, the kind that only the Divine Owner can fill us with, to assure we will operate in the right mode in which He designed us. The only fuel that will work to get us running as generators of something divine is, as the Bible says, "every Word that comes from God's mouth" (Deut. 8:3; Luke 4:4).

In God's Word, in Colossians 3:16, Paul implores his readers to "let the Word of Christ dwell in you richly." It's as if he is stating that when you make the choice to take in God's Word as a daily part of your existence and allow it to soak into your being, it increasingly becomes a part of who you are (or better yet, allows you to become more like who He is).

Remember that saying "You are what you eat"? When you consume and digest God's Word, it starts to fuel and empower the very fabric of your being.

So, my fellow generators, how is the spiritual fuel supply in your life these days?

THE BURNING BUSH

Read Exodus Chapter 3.

Consider Moses in the desert when he encountered God in the miraculous burning bush. It was the spark of God's presence that ignited that bush! That same spark of God led Moses to do His will in leading the Israelites out of slavery and on the road to the Promised Land.

The lesson: we need the spark of God's presence to lead us to live the life and do the work to which He has called us.

Spark

Finally, the generator needs the spark of an outside source to initiate the process that enables it to run. A generator can't start itself. It needs the pull or applied energy of the owner to bring it to life. Once the owner's power initiates the generator, the machine begins to produce a current the owner can use to help accomplish his purposes. But it all starts with the power of the owner's hand.

For people, the one and only spark that ignites us to worship and serve God comes from His Spirit. It is only through His Holy Spirit that we have both the spark of eternal life that empowers us to generate great lives for God and the "oil of God" that keeps us refreshed and operating in His strength and not our own. Paul again implores us in Colossians 3:15 to "let the peace of Christ rule in your hearts." Unlike a generator, we have to choose to let God's spark of the Holy Spirit be at the very center of our being. When this happens, the Holy Spirit will activate the "Word" fuel within us to generate the powerful current of a life empowered by God.

Spark and fuel work together in a generator to produce electrical current whenever the owner brings it to life.

When God's Word and Holy Spirit are activated in our lives, we not only experience His power, we also become conduits and instruments through which God's power is revealed to other people. Worship happens when we allow God to fuel and ignite us, and then we are available for Him to use as He calls us for His purposes.

Chapter 20

WINESKINS

The actual experience of authentic, God-empowered worship always matters more than the forms of worship we use. Don't get me wrong; it's not that God can't be experienced in rituals, liturgies, or other traditions or forms that come under the category "the way we've always done it." It's just that sometimes the way we worship can end up meaning more to us than actually meeting God in worship. When this happens, we need to honestly and prayerfully assess our attitudes and practices.

Jesus used the parable of the wineskin to illustrate the truth about this. Consider His words:

[People don't] pour new wine into old wineskins. If they do, the skins will burst; the wine will run out and the wineskins will be ruined. No, they pour new wine into new wineskins, and both are preserved. (Matt. 9:17)

The wineskins to which Jesus referred were the typical and often-used containers of His time, made from a whole, skinned goat whose limbs and neck were cut off and then sealed. The wine, once poured inside this nearly airtight vessel, would continue to ferment. The resulting carbon dioxide stretched the goatskin nearly to the point of breaking until the wine was poured out and the goatskin relaxed. Over and over the goatskin vessel would be filled, stretched, and then relaxed until it eventually lost its ability to carry liquid. Then it would burst, or develop cracks that rendered it useless to carry any of the precious liquid. A new wineskin had to be made to hold the new wine it was made to carry. In other words, the vessel only matters as long as it works to hold what's really important: the wine.

New Wineskins

Jesus's point was simply this: any religious tradition, regulation, or worship form that no longer leads people to experience the living God is like a leaky or broken container trying to hold brand-new wine. It can't be done. When our religious systems and forms no longer hold the wine of the God's presence, we need to adapt, change, or even abandon the tradition or form that is broken and replace it with something that invites and carries God's presence and is true to His Word.

It doesn't matter if it is an old tradition or a new one, a personal preference or a dyed-in-the-wool church practice. If God no longer inhabits our worship, we need to adapt or discard the form and worship God in a fresh way prompted by His Word and filled with His Holy Spirit. Simply going through the motions of worship is not only sad, but also dangerous. There is the danger we will value the form of something in which we once experienced God over God Himself. The Israelites once fell into this when they began to worship the flowering staff of Moses as an object, rather than simply remembering to worship God *alone* who once revealed His power through the budding staff. Their misplaced worship resulted in their alienation from God and opened the door to a host of other problems. The same can happen to us.

We would do well to remember that God-given change is good. God's Word reminds us that soon Jesus will come again and change *everything*. As He says, "Behold, I am making everything new!" (Rev. 21:5). I am not suggesting we discard the great hymns of our faith or throw out any tradition that comes from God and still draws more and more people to God. I am not suggesting that any church adopt a practice outside the parameters of God's Word.

We would be wise, however, to remember that Psalm 95 tells us to sing a new song to the Lord. The admonition here is to have the freshness of worship alive in our praises of God. There should be nothing stale or half-hearted when we worship the King of Kings. New songs, as well as fresh arrangements of hymns, are to be encouraged and not stifled. This has been the way of the church since the beginning, and God is worthy of this kind of worship each time we come before Him as individuals and as a church.

Change and Renewal

God can use the challenges of change to shape our hearts and renew our minds as we approach Him in worship—if we allow Him to do so. An eighty-year-old woman at our church recently told me that after years of struggling with changes in worship music, she asked God to speak to her and change her heart, and now she "is worshipping God like never before!"

On the other hand, for some people the idea of any kind of change in Christian worship is tantamount to heresy. Case in point: an angry woman called our church office a while back and offered to make a huge donation if the church threw out all contemporary music and went back to only the traditional music to which she was accustomed and enjoyed.

(For the record, this church used both contemporary and traditional music in worship.) The office manager who fielded the call declined her offer and politely told her the church doesn't accept "strings-attached" gifts or act in ways contrary to the direction that our leadership has prayerfully discerned God is leading our church.

To be sure, there are non-negotiables in our faith. God's Word never changes, and everything we say and do must be both empowered by His Holy Spirit and in line with the full context of His Word.

So, the message never changes. But the way we communicate the message—the music, preaching style, and other elements of public worship—must be adaptable and accessible to the many different cultures and generations that comprise the body of Christ. Even as the Apostle Paul never varied from the Gospel message, he clearly presented it using two unique styles to two different people groups at a synagogue and public square in Athens, Greece. To the Athenian Jews, who knew the Old Testament, he used Old Testament scriptures to present Christ as the prophesied Messiah. To the non-Jewish, secular Athenians, Paul began his presentation of the Good News of Jesus by reminding the people of the words on a monument in their city:

For as I walked around and looked carefully at your objects of worship, I even found an altar with this inscription: To an unknown god. So you are ignorant of the very thing you worship—and this is what I am going to proclaim to you. (Acts 17:23)

Varying Styles of Worship

God-honoring worship that is adaptable to the culture has been the pattern of the church since the first century, as is chronicled in this article:

The musical forms of early Christian worship were initially Jewish, such as the chanting of Psalms. As the Gentile missions began, Christians began incorporating Greek music forms. The language of worship became almost universally Greek, which was the common language of the Roman Empire, and more and more Greek music forms and theory came into use in the Church. Within twenty to forty years, the Christian worship service was a composite of Jewish and Greek liturgical music forms, following the basic shape of Jewish Synagogue and Temple worship. Within a hundred years, as the Church spread across the Roman Empire and most of its members were Gentiles who spoke Greek and lived in a Greek culture, most of the musical style and theory had become Greek. (Williams)

It is the same today with worship music styles. I have had the privilege of leading worship all over the world and am thrilled to have worshipped with the exuberant joy of music from Africa as well as the rich hymns from Russia. I have led worship using edgier worship music that draws on electric guitars and a band (see Psalm 150) and have led seniors in worship using a piano and hymns. All of these musical styles can give glory to God—as long as He, not the musical style, is the focus.

Charles Finney was a famous evangelist who lived in the 1800s. In an 1835 publication entitled *Lectures on Revival*, he wrote about the reactions of many churches to changes in worship. This article sheds light on the ongoing tensions between accepted traditions and innovations in worship nearly two centuries ago.

Finney wrote on changes in pastors' clothing during worship:

Our present forms of public worship—all the facets of the way we do things—have developed piece by piece through a succession of new measures . . . Many years ago pastors always wore special clothing . . . a cocked hat, clerical bands instead of a necktie or scarf, small clothes and a wig . . . These things were customary, and every cleric was obligated to wear them. All of these habits had no doubt developed through a series of innovations, for we have no good reason to believe that the apostles and early ministers dressed any differently from anyone else. When tradition changed, the church cried out as if some divine institution had been struck down.

When pastors began to wear neckties or scarves rather than clerical bands, Finney wrote, "churchgoers charged that they were becoming irreligious. In some places a pastor wouldn't dare to be seen in the pulpit in a necktie."

On new worship music in the church in 1835:

Once it was customary to sing David's psalms. In time, along came a version of the Psalms in rhyme . . . When pastors sought to introduce them, churches were distracted, people violently opposed, and great trouble was created by the invention . . . finally [now famous hymn writer] Isaac Watts wrote his version, which was still opposed in many churches a century after its introduction. People in numerous congregations continue to walk out of church if a psalm or hymn is taught from a new book.

On the introduction of choirs in worship, Finney wrote the following:

Later it was thought best to have select singers sit by themselves and sing to help improve the music. This was bitterly opposed. Many congregations split over the desire of pastors and some leaders to cultivate music by forming choirs. People thought great evil was coming to the church because singers sat by themselves and cultivated music and learned new tunes the old people couldn't sing.

Churches were deeply divided over the introduction of the organ in worship:

Some congregations brought in instruments to help the singers and improve the music. [These things] . . . caused commotion . . . a certain church had an organ in their building. They wouldn't get half as upset to be told sinners are going to hell than to be told someone is installing an organ in the meeting house.

Finney summed up his article with this insight:

Why couldn't these customs be given up without producing a shock? People felt they could hardly worship God without them—but plainly their attachment was no part of true Christianity. It was mere superstition. (Charles Finney, Lectures on Revival)

It's illuminating to see these things in hindsight, as they now seem frivolous and a bit humorous. It's even more important for each of us to take an inventory of our own set of worship dos and don'ts in this same light to see if we are reacting in the same way.

Sing a New Song

Psalm 96 states we are to "sing to the Lord a new song." God enjoys freshness in our worship expression. When you think about it, all the songs and hymns we sing were at one time a new song to the church, and many of them were initially criticized as too innovative or different. Even the great hymn "Amazing Grace" was early criticized by a scholar as not being an example of the better work of writer John Newton. I wonder what that scholar would say today.

Let us remember that God, who inspired those writers, is the same God who is inspiring today's worship composers. As we approach God in worship, let's ask Him to steer our minds and hearts to Him alone and away from anything we would construct apart from Him as a precondition to worshipping Him. Let's thank Him for the gift of worship, music, and the new songs He is giving to the church.

William Booth, founder of the Salvation Army, summarized it best when he wrote the following:

Music has a divine effect upon divinely influenced and directed souls. Music is to the soul what the wind is to the ship, blowing her onward in the direction in which she is steered . . . Not allowed to sing that tune or this tune? Indeed! Secular music, do you say? Belongs to the devil does it? Well, if it did, I would plunder him of it, for he has no right to a single note of the whole seven. But we deny it. He's the thief . . . Every note and every strain and every harmony is divine and belongs to us . . . So consecrate your voices and your instruments. Bring out your cornets, and harps, and organs, and flutes and violins, and pianos, and drums, and everything else that can make melody! Offer them to God and use them to make all the hearts about you merry before the Lord. (Booth)

As individuals and as a church, we need to continually and prayerfully ask God to show us the external areas of our lives and worship that have become ineffective, leaky containers that no longer carry the wine of His holy presence. More than seeking the comfort of the familiar, we should seek the presence of God, even if He is revealing Himself in something new to us. God is able to fill us with the peace and comfort of His presence—even in that which may initially be unfamiliar and uncomfortable to us.

Finally, let us never forget the ultimate worship celebration happens when lost, soul-weary people experience the joy of a whole new life in Jesus Christ. May our worship of God always invite more people to experience Jesus Christ in a life-changing way. All of heaven rejoices when this happens.

—— Reflections on Experiencing God in Worship ——

The essence of worship is to experience God and be changed.

Perspectives

What are your first-thought perspectives and reflections on experiencing God in worship? What strikes you as important, interesting, or challenging?

Foundations

How do you "experience God in worship"? In what ways might this be about asking and receiving? In what ways might this be about acknowledging and responding?

God is seeking true worshipers. Has He found one in you? Review and reflect on the heart-check questions in the chapter "God-Directed Worship."

Insights

The essence of worship is to experience God and be changed. This occurs both in our personal time with God and when we gather with others in God-directed and empowered worship.

When you experience God, how do you begin to change in your spirit, emotions, intellect, will, and body? In what new ways do you feel, think, speak, and act as a conduit of praise?

Being filled with the Spirit (Eph. 5:18) is synonymous with letting the word of Christ dwell within you richly (Col. 3:16). How are you doing when it comes to practicing this?

Application

How do you see Part 4's "Experiencing" insights as challenging, changing, or reinforcing your perspectives and experience? How are you being called closer to God in worship?

Are you or others around you having trouble with current wineskins of your worship experience? Why? What are some steps that can be taken?

How are you "singing a new song" these days?

PART 5

LIVING A LIFE OF WORSHIP

Our encounter with God leads to an everyday life of worship.

It is confirmed and activated as we respond to His call to do His kingdom work on earth and live each day and moment as an act of worship for Him.

Like Isaiah, we raise our hand and passionately plead, "Here I am. Send me!"

Chapter 21

A NEW ROUTE: REPENTANCE

Worship becomes real and activated in our lives when it moves from the realm of an event into the reality of personal transformation. Isaiah's worship of God moved from the venue of the heavenly throne room to the dusty roads and crowded cities of the Israelites when his life was put on a new trajectory through his encounter with God.

This is the non-negotiable of worship: once you truly meet with God, the path of your life can never be the same again. Think about it. If you have had an encounter with God, how could life ever be the same again? Either you will run away from God or follow God in every aspect of your life. There is no middle ground.

The Magi and the Christ Child

Another example of how God changes the path of people's lives occurred shortly after Jesus was born. In the account of Jesus's birth in the Gospel of Matthew, the Magi from the region of what is now Iraq saw all the signs that the Messiah was to be born. Being scholars and God-seekers, they decided to take an extended field trip to find this king and actually worship Him (Matt. 2:2). Their search led them into Jerusalem, the capital city of Israel, where as respected visitors they went through all the proper political channels, including an audience with King Herod. What the Magi didn't know was that Herod would try to use the knowledge they gained in order to find the exact location of the Messiah to kill Him and ensure his own reign as king. He asked them to come back with a report on the newborn king's location and baited them with the lie that he also wanted to "go and worship him" (verse 8).

As they went on their way, they finally encountered Jesus. Take a look at what then took place:

1. They bowed to and worshipped the Christ child. What a mind-boggling experience this must have been to Mary, Joseph, and bystanders to see these learned and respected scholars praising, singing, praying to, and totally submitting themselves to this young child. For the Magi, they didn't just see a child, they saw the fulfillment of an ancient prophecy: God in the flesh. The wise men didn't care what anyone else thought; they simply and unashamedly worshipped God.

2. They opened their travel cases, a bit like today's suitcases, wallets, and purses, and presented Jesus with gifts of gold, incense, and myrrh. In this way, they backed up their voices of worship with lavish acts of worship that cost them quite a bit financially. This is a lesson for Christ-followers today, for us to "put our money where our mouth is" in giving to God's kingdom work. Incidentally, I've often wondered if the expensive gifts the Magi gave helped Joseph and Mary cover their travel and housing expenses when God directed them to flee with Jesus to Egypt.

3. The Magi paid attention to and followed God's warning in a dream not to go back to Herod. They knew God was leading them and decided to listen and follow His prompts, even if His instructions came in a dream.

4. In obedience to God's leading in that dream, they went home a different way than they came. The Bible states they went home to their own country by a different route.

A New Way

Going home another way: this is a key characteristic of worship activated in our lives as well. If we have met God in worship, the following are true:

- We are forgiven and set free from our past mistakes and sins.
- We are given a new start and a new position as God's adopted and loved daughter or son in Jesus Christ.
- We are healed of our spiritual, psychological, and sometimes even physical disorders.
- We are infused with His own Holy Spirit to equip and empower us to live for Him.

Then how could we ever go back to the old route of our life?

When Jesus forgave people their sins, He also told them to go and sin no more. When we truly encounter Jesus and experience His divine forgiveness and intervention, we also need to hear His voice telling us to step away from the sin, attitudes, behaviors, and lifestyle we previously chose and to walk a new and different path with Him. This is the very definition of repentance. "Going home another way" means so much more than just wanting to feel better about our past life. It really means we are ready to go the way God wants us to go.

Just like Herod, the old ruling patterns and relationships of our lives are demented powers that will deceive and destroy us and others if we go back to them. But when we have really tasted and experienced God, He will point us to a new way of going home to Him, a healthy and fulfilling way that leads to life both now and into eternity.

Worship activated means going through life on a new and different route. Are you ready to receive and travel on God's new path for your life?

Chapter 22

ALLEGIANCE

What Will They Think?

H ave you ever wondered this: what will people think of me if I start talking about Jesus and my faith?

I have heard these words spoken by other people, and I've entertained that same thought in my own mind. At some point in his life, Isaiah probably asked himself the same question, but he went ahead and boldly spoke for God. The source of the "what-will-people-think?" question is the voice of self-centered, me-focused fear. And fear is a big obstacle to offering a life of real worship to God.

Speaking out on God's behalf didn't create an easy life for Isaiah. He spent around forty-four years of his life prophesying to people who didn't listen to him. From the beginning, God made it clear to Isaiah that this would happen, but still told him to speak on His behalf to

His people. So how did Isaiah move beyond his fear into boldness? I believe Isaiah's allegiance to God overruled and overwhelmed any fear or obstacle that confronted him. Allegiance is an important component in living a life of worship to God.

Committed Allegiance

Worship is all about allegiance. We cannot fully worship God if we haven't pledged and aren't truly living our allegiance to Him alone. This allegiance stands above anything else in life, including our life and security, our jobs, our hopes and dreams, our residency, and even our loved ones. Jesus made this abundantly clear:

> Anyone who loves father or mother more than me is not worthy of me; anyone who loves son or daughter more than me is not worthy of me. (Matt. 10:37)

Jesus's point wasn't that we stop loving the loved ones He has blessed us with, but that we always put our relationship with God above anyone or anything in this life. Remember the rich young ruler who left Jesus because he couldn't let go of his first allegiance, his wealth? It's easy to see what was more important to him. His first allegiance was given to something other than God. Augustine wrote, "Christ is not valued at all unless He be valued above all."

When we value what other people think of us over our allegiance to God, we are putting our allegiance in them and not in Him. Allegiance to God includes putting your relationship with God above everything else, including what other people may think of you. Jesus told us that love-allegiance to Him has a necessary condition. In John's Gospel, Jesus makes a remarkable if-then statement:

> If a person really loves Me, he will obey My teaching; and My Father will love him, and We will come to him and make Our home with him. Anyone who does not really love Me does not observe and obey My teaching. (John 14:23–24)

Allegiance to Jesus involves so much more than worshipping with other Christ-followers, although that is very important. An authentic allegiance to Jesus Christ inherently means we will do what He tells us to do—not just in the romanticized, easy-to-serve moments, but in the tough, hard-to-go-on times when His Word is the only thing we can depend on. Why? Because we *love* Him and are committed to Him above everything and everyone else. The condition of allegiance is to bring the Good News of Jesus to everyone. If we love Jesus, we are compelled to do what He tells us to do. He left no doubt as to what He asks of us:

> Go then and make disciples of all the nations, baptizing them in the name of the Father and of the Son and of the Holy Spirit, teaching them to observe everything that I have commanded you. (Matt. 28:20)

Trying harder or striving to be committed to God in our own power can't generate allegiance to Him. True allegiance comes out of experiencing God. When we have a real, transformed relationship with God, His love will compel us to move beyond our fears. When we deeply experience God, we will move more and more into a worshipful life of allegiance to Him. A sign of this allegiance is that we increasingly do what God tells us to do when He tells us to do it.

LIFE-LONG ALLEGIANCE
Read Genesis 6:9–22.

Noah's allegiance to God meant disregarding and enduring contempt and mocking from his neighbors while he followed God in what appeared to be a crazy scheme of building a huge ark. His allegiance resulted in life for his family and for generations who came after him.

The Lesson: life-long allegiance to Jesus Christ is an essential component of our faith walk.

Lived Obedience

Jesus said the real evidence of our love for Him is this: we obey Him. And what does He command? He requires that we tell other people about Him and then walk beside them until they become fully equipped, Spirit-filled Christ-followers.

We can profess to worship God, but if we are not living our love for God in a life that willingly obeys his directives, we are not fully worshipping Him. Pretty tough words, huh? How can we ever live up to this massive, overwhelming task when we are such flawed and puny people?

As with all worship, allegiance to God can only happen in His power, not in our own. The reality is that God is the author of faithful allegiance. He will never leave us to hang out to dry without hope, because He promised He would always be with us—and in us. We simply can't do anything of kingdom work on our own, but only in the power of the Holy Spirit, who enables us to successfully do the work that He has put before us.

In Acts 4 we find Peter and John in front of the same religious leaders who in the not-too-distant past had condemned Jesus to die on the cross. Peter and John were brought before the council because they prayed in the name of Jesus over a man crippled from birth, and the man was healed. When asked by the high priests by what power they performed this healing, Peter boldly spoke. Yes, Peter, the same one who, only months earlier, had denied Christ three times, now eloquently told the tribunal about Jesus, the risen Son of God, in these words:

> Rulers and elders of the people! If we are being called to account today for an act of kindness shown to a man who was lame and are being asked how he was healed, then know this, you and all the people of Israel: It is by the name of Jesus Christ of Nazareth, whom you crucified but whom God raised from the dead, that this man stands before you healed. Jesus is 'the stone you builders rejected, which has become the cornerstone'. Salvation is found in no one else, for there is no other name under heaven given to mankind by which we must be saved. (Acts 4:8–12)

What caused the change in Peter? There is a clue in this section of the Bible that makes it clear how Peter could speak so boldly to the leaders who could have ordered his imprisonment or death:

> Peter, filled with the Holy Spirit, said to them. (Acts 4:8)

The Holy Spirit, the very power of Jesus Christ, was the source of their power because He was now with them and *in* them. When threatened by the religious leaders and told not to talk about Jesus, Peter and John told the council that they couldn't stop talking about Jesus because they had to tell others about what they saw and heard and experienced. Peter's love for the One who saved Him compelled Him to speak, and the power of the Holy Spirit within Him empowered Him to do so.

I have no idea what people God will ask of you to present Jesus, but I'm sure He will ask you. By our consistent and grace-filled lives, by genuine acts of love and service, and by our obedient willingness to share our story and offer the Good News of Jesus in the power of God, we will activate and offer the most amazing worship offering to God: our very lives.

Chapter 23

UNITY

I n the fall of 1987, I got a call from my brother-in-law asking me if I wanted to go to a Minnesota Twins game with him that night. This was an amazing opportunity because it was not just any game, it was an American League Championship game. In an exciting game, the Twins ended up winning, ultimately propelling them to win the World Series. I will never forget being part the massive crowd that cheered at ear-splitting levels (my ears were ringing for three days), waved "homer hankies," and high-fived each other even as we walked the streets to our cars after the game. In that moment, it felt like we were one, united and celebrating together in a common experience. Our team had won, and it felt great.

Exhilarating, Unifying, Enduring

Now multiply this by a million or more. This is the kind of experience God wants for us as Christ-followers: an exhilarating, unifying, and enduring sense that we all belong to God's winning team. Unlike baseball teams, this unity doesn't fade or vanish with the years. In fact, it can and will get better if we say yes to God's vision and plan for unity in our family, groups, and churches.

To be clear, unity is not an end in itself. Unity for unity's sake alone is dangerous and can even cause us to be bound to others who might not care about God but are more interested in advancing their agendas. Instead, Jesus shows us the real purpose for unity: so that Christ-followers, by our togetherness, will be effective in demonstrating to our planet that Jesus is the Son of God, the Savior and Redeemer of the world. In John 17:20–21, Jesus prayed the following prayer to the Father for us, His church:

> My prayer is not for them alone. I pray also for those who will believe in me through their message, that all of them may be one, Father, just as you are in me and I am in you. May they also be in us so that the world may believe that you have sent me.

Unity is not some superficial truce or tense pact with others. It can't be generated by human effort alone. Rather, it is a deep, abiding gift from God; it's a sense of oneness that reconciles and overrides our differences, tastes, preferences, and even worship styles. Even as it is God-given, we must still choose unity over division and live it in our shared life with other Christians. Psalm 133 tells us real, covenantal unity is the conduit through which God pours out His Spirit and blessings on the church:

> How good and pleasant it is when God's people live together in unity! It is like precious oil poured on the head, running down on the beard, running down on Aaron's beard, down on the collar of his robe. It is as if the dew

of Hermon were falling on Mount Zion. For there the Lord bestows his blessing, even life forevermore.

Experiencing God is not only a "God-and-me" individual encounter, although there is a definite need for this. God also desires for us to know Him in a deep, new way as we live and worship with others who have also given their lives to Christ. The amazing promise of Psalm 133 is that God will bestow His lavish blessings on the people who live together in unity for Him.

When we yield our differences to God and make the choice to love and honor each other in godly unity, the "oil" of God's presence will drench us from head to toe, bathing us in His presence. Thicker than dew on the most humid summer day, God's blessings will surround us until we have a taste of what it will be like someday in His eternal presence. The world will begin to take notice as well. Unity is a powerful act of worship that requires both God's intervention and our decisions as individuals and a group to honor him and live together in harmony.

Brokenness United

A few years ago, I helped lead worship at a large international ministry conference in Budapest, Hungary. Each day I met with worship leaders from a different country, learned a worship song from their delegation, and later taught it to the entire gathering as part of evening worship. One of the most exhilarating worship experiences I have ever had came one night after I led everyone in a powerful and deep worship song I learned from a former Eastern Bloc country. As we finished the song, two men from this country came forward to the microphone. They explained, through interpreters, that they knew each other from the past: one was a Christian pastor imprisoned for His faith; the other was his prison guard. It turned out they rediscovered each other at the conference. What could have been a painful or ugly scene was instead an emotional and beautiful encounter. You see, after the pastor was released, his former guard had come to faith in Christ. These two men now wept and hugged each other, not as enemies but as newfound brothers in Christ. It was such a powerful display of reconciliation that the entire gathering spontaneously formed a *huge* circle and began worshipping and singing in many different languages. It was like Pentecost all over again. God's presence was noticeably and powerfully felt, like dew, in the room. This still impacts my life many years later because it reminds me how God shows up when we are truly united in Him.

Unity happens when we decide to lay down the arms of division and accusation and instead choose to seek God and yield to Him as we work through our dissonances and disagreements. When this happens, be ready for God's deepest anointing and blessing.

Today, as you reflect on unity, ask God to create in you a heart for the kind of unity He alone can produce. Make a commitment to pray for God's unity in your family, group, or church, and pray specifically for the people God lays on your heart. Fair warning: these may be the very people you've had the hardest time being around! Finally, as you worship today, you may want to pray to be the kind of person Francis of Assisi prayed to be:

Lord, make me an instrument of your peace.

Where there is hatred, let me sow love;

Where there is injury, pardon;

Where there is doubt, faith;

Where there is despair, hope;

Where there is darkness, light;

And where there is sadness, joy.

Chapter 24

MOPS AND GATES

Mops

You might encounter Vern if you come into the building during the afternoon hours at my home church. Vern will be quietly and cheerfully pushing a mop through the empty coffee shop that bustles with people on Sundays and some weeknights. If he's not cleaning up the coffee shop floor, you'll probably find him mopping a hallway or stairs. Vern always has a friendly word and a smile for anyone who comes his way. Vern has this infectious, almost-boyish laugh that makes you want to smile and join in. There is something so inviting about Vern that you look forward to the next time you'll see him. At first glance you would think Vern is a paid employee of the church simply doing his job.

You would be wrong.

Here's the real deal: Vern *gives* his time to serve. He and his wife Barb volunteer as a way of giving something back to God and the people of their church. Their service comes out of their deep sense of joy and gratefulness that is readily apparent to anyone who meets them. Their giving is not done reluctantly or begrudgingly, but springs out of who they are and what they believe.

Vern's mop is a powerful witness to me, which brings me to the idea of Thanksgiving.

Thanksgiving

Most Americans associate Thanksgiving with the November day when we gather around a table with family and friends to eat, talk, watch football, and figure out what ungodly hour we will wake up to go to the Black Friday shopping event the next morning.

Don't get me wrong. There is nothing inherently wrong with eating and gathering together. But for most of us, this annual rite has a roughly thirty-second, perfunctory Thanksgiving meal prayer before we dive into the important stuff: the food. Sometimes it can feel this day has become more about Thanks-taking than Thanks-giving.

Vern has shown me what real thanksgiving is all about. The dictionary defines thanksgiving as "the act of giving thanks; grateful acknowledgment of benefits or favors, especially to God." Please note in this definition that there is an *action* involved. Thanksgiving is not a passive, nebulous notion. Thanksgiving calls us to recall what we have been blessed with and then act on or give back what springs out of the gratefulness in our heart.

The very act of giving thanks, it seems to me, has to come out of a profound sense that we have been *given* something of such value or worth that we are compelled in the deepest part of our being to give our deep appreciation to the Giver.

In other words, giving follows thanks.

At one point in Jesus's earthly ministry, He came across ten lepers. The scourge of their society, these infected outcasts dared to ask Jesus to heal them. Luke 17 tells us Jesus heard them and instructed them to go show themselves to the local Jewish temple priests, as these were the only ones who could verify the lepers were healed and re-certify them back into society. On the way to showing themselves to the religious leaders, *all* ten lepers were healed—all skin sores and physical conditions cleansed, healed, and removed. After showing themselves to the shocked religious leaders—and presumably being given permission to reenter a world they were banned from for days, months, or years—nine of them slipped into obscurity, never to see Jesus again.

Only one returned to Jesus; he was a Samaritan. This guy was an outcast, not only because of his disease, but also because of his background and heritage. He was essentially a double outcast. The Jewish people of that day despised Samaritans, considering them half-breeds who had assimilated with and bonded to non-Jewish peoples. So this outcast of outcasts came running back to Jesus. With loud, heartfelt praises to God, he flung himself at Jesus's feet and profusely thanked Him. Why? Because, more than anyone else, this man *knew* the depth of what had been given to him, and he had to *give* Jesus a lavish expression of what flowed out of his heart. He couldn't help but give thanks.

After pointing out that this foreign Samaritan was the only one of the ten to come back with thanks and praise to God, Jesus lovingly told the man, "Rise and go; your faith has made you well" (Luke 17:19). I suspect this man went out and told many people in that region about what Jesus had done for him, because this was part of his giving thanks.

Gates

We are all like lepers in life. All of us are outcasts from God until we cry out to Jesus to do what we can't do ourselves: make us spiritually whole, forgiven, and healed of the leprous sores of sin that have permeated our very being. Jesus's answer to our cries is always *yes*. When we allow Jesus in, we are no longer foreigners or strangers to God, but healed, redeemed, and welcomed sons and daughters who now belong to God forever. The depth of our gratitude grows by ocean fathoms when we comprehend just how much Jesus has done for us. When we come to this place, it's time to let the King of Glory in:

> Lift up your heads, O gates; and be lifted up, O ancient doors, that the King of glory may come in!
>
> Who is the King of glory? The Lord strong and mighty, the Lord mighty in battle.
>
> Lift up your heads, O gates, and lift them up, O ancient doors, that the King of glory may come in! (Ps. 24:7–9, NASB)

The reality of God-worship activated in your life is simply to open the doors and gates of your heart to the only One who perfectly understands you, perfectly loves you, and will perfectly fulfill and complete you: Jesus Christ.

The "gates" in this psalm were the access points that led people to the temple of Jerusalem, where the symbol of God's presence—the ark of the covenant—was housed. The ark of the covenant was the sign of God's provision, His covenant relationship, and His protection of the Jewish people. It was also a symbol of a much better temple that was to come and is already here.

Living out worship in your life involves opening your innermost being and letting in the King of Glory, Jesus Christ. This means that we can actually become a temple of the Holy Spirit, housing God's presence, which will always be with us and carry us through eternity.

The evidence of our relationship with the Lord Jesus Christ is found in the choices we make and the kind of lives we live. Whenever our Good Shepherd directs us to do something practical for the least among us, it's time to "sheep-up" and obediently follow Him and do as He says. If our worship life does not compel us to care for the least among us, perhaps it's time to reassess if we have truly given God full access to our hearts and lives.

Caring "for the least of these" (Matt. 25:40) may mean taking time to regularly visit a senior who is lonely or in failing health. It may involve adopting a child in a third world country through a regular, monthly gift to a reputable hunger-relief organization. It may mean writing a letter to a legislator about an injustice in the world. God may even be calling you to move to a different neighborhood, city, state, or foreign country and spend your days helping people to see who Jesus really is through practical, tangible ministry or relief efforts.

Activating Worship

Worship is activated when we show Jesus-generated love to those who are in trouble, are downcast, or in need. This kind of worship expression flows out of the realization that Jesus rescued us out of our desperate condition. We are no different than those He calls us to serve, but simply come from different circumstances. When we have encountered God in a life-altering deliverance, we no longer live the way we used to live. Something fundamental and foundational changes in us. Our very nature is tied to God.

This is the activation of a lifetime of real worship.

Opening the door in Christ-directed worship in our churches also requires that we continually seek God and open ourselves to Him. It's time for the gates and doors of our churches to be flung open as we do these acts of worship:

- Offering our hearts to pray for and serve each other and our community
- Welcoming Christ-followers of all ages, races, and cultures, rather than confining the church to the people group we feel most comfortable around
- Opening our hearts and minds to God's Word and fresh call for the church, letting go of individual agendas and preconceived notions, ready to listen to and follow God's leading for our fellowship
- Opening our doors to lost, hurting, and searching people who don't look or dress like us, who nevertheless come into our churches looking for God and answers to their life and circumstances
- Opening our vision to see our church in the bigger picture of God's kingdom, rather than focusing on parochialism, denominationalism, or minor personal differences that the enemy would leverage to divide Christ-followers
- Opening ourselves to going out the doors of our church to love and serve others and bring Christ to them, rather than sit and wonder why more people aren't coming to our church

When this becomes the abiding reality of the church, we will see the doors of more people's hearts being flung open to Christ.

And we will hear Jesus's voice telling us to rise and go. That's the time when real worship and thanksgiving begins. We don't need to disappear into spiritual obscurity, but can gratefully *give* from the *thanks* that flows from our hearts, telling other people what Jesus has done for us, going and serving wherever and whenever God asks us.

Even if that means picking up a mop.

Chapter 25
PERSEVERING

n my high school track days, I used to run the 1,600-meter event, which is roughly equivalent to one mile. This race is accomplished by running four full laps around a 400-meter track. In my short track and field career, I had some success in this event, even though I chose high school musicals and a rock band over track as I progressed through high school. I still enjoy running on a regular basis, including training and participating in running events. One year my oldest daughter and I trained for and completed the Minneapolis half-marathon, along with a few thousand other runners. To my shock, I later discovered I took fifth place for my age group.

There is an interesting phenomenon that I experienced and have observed in running that has a lot to do with pressing on in hard or uncertain times. You would think the hardest, most mentally challenging part of any race would be the final leg of the race, but my experience has led me to believe otherwise. In the 1,600-meter, a fast-paced, adrenaline-fueled rush among the runners marks the initial lap. The runners still have some of this energy pushing them through the second lap. It is the third lap, the one in which the end is still not in sight but the energy of the start of the race has faded, that separates the elite runners from the rest of the pack. This is the lap that marks the best-trained and most-disciplined runners. They push through this lap with enough stamina to hear the bell signaling the final lap, one in which they can go for the finish line with their final kick.

My track coach taught me that a good race is all about training, personal pacing, and sticking to a disciplined plan over the roller coaster of fatigue and physical discomfort during a race. He was there to train me, cheer me on during the race, and correct me afterwards so I could do even better in future races.

An aspect of activating our worship of God that sometimes goes undetected is perseverance. The dictionary defines perseverance as "steadfastness in doing something despite difficulty or delay in achieving success, or continuance in a state of grace leading finally to a state of glory." Being steadfast, continuing on in God all the way to a state of glory, this is worship lived out in our life.

Yet I Will Rejoice

Persevering as an expression of worship doesn't come from some notion we have to tough it out on our own. We'll only end up tired and discouraged if we attempt this in our own strength. God-given perseverance springs out of the deep inner sense that no matter what we go through in life, God hasn't left us. He loves us, will never leave us, and has a bigger plan that marches on, uninterrupted by unexpected or threatening circumstances. Finally, He has included us in His big plan and promises the end of our story is a happy and victorious one.

To illustrate this, in the third chapter of Habakkuk, the writer paints a dark and dismal picture of what was happening in his life. He lives in a country devastated by war and occupation. Fear has been his companion, and he is tempted to give in to the black hole of despair. As a farmer and rancher, the worst-case scenario has happened: There is no fruit on any of the fig trees or grape vines. The olive crop has failed. All his sheep have died in the field, and his cattle barns are empty. But then, out of the blue, he makes this amazing statement:

Yet I will rejoice in the Lord! I will be joyful in God my Savior! The Sovereign Lord is my strength! He makes my feet like the feet of a deer; he enables me to tread on the heights. (Hab. 3:18–19)

The writer of Habakkuk understood that God is still God even in dark times, so he made the conscious choice to worship God above and beyond what he was currently experiencing. He made the choice to speak this truth aloud in the midst of the ugliness around him. He planted his flag of faith in the ground and chose to move forward toward God's intended future in God's power, rather than remain stuck in the temporary, present circumstances.

It's easy to worship God in smooth times, when every day seems sunny and pleasant. It's quite another thing to praise Him in the middle of a storm, one that lasts for months or even years. When an illness strikes you or someone you love, when death brings a sad silence to a home, when the economic rug gets pulled out from underneath us through unemployment or financial losses, or when someone leaves you high and dry, it can feel the world is coming to an end.

But because of God, your story doesn't end there. Even through tears, we can worship God from wherever we are because He is still taking us to a glorious future just beyond our sight. We can persevere with God because He still holds us in the palm of His hand. He will take us, step by step, to a place that will one day cause us to look at hard times as nothing compared to the amazing glory and exhilaration we then experience.

People who keep going forward with God through the hard times of life also develop an inner spiritual discipline, a willingness to grow and learn, and a sustainable personal pace. These are the ones who emerge intact at the end of the tough times. Through the hard times of life, they learn this truth: "God blesses those who patiently endure testing and temptation. Afterward they will receive the crown of life that God has promised to those who love him" (James 1:12).

Running the Good Race

Persevering becomes an act of worship as we both speak and live out our trust in God. To persevere with God, it's important to have a network of Christ-followers as a support team to help you, cheer you on, and bring grace and truth as you press on in God's course for your life. These people will be your cheerleaders and witnesses to God's faithfulness, as the scripture states: "Since we are surrounded by such a great cloud of witnesses, let us throw off everything that hinders and the sin that so easily entangles, and let us run with perseverance the race marked out for us" (Heb. 12:1).

Worship God and look to His strength as you continue running the race of life, even when the finish line isn't yet in sight and you don't feel the energy you had when you first started. Jesus promised us there's a fantastic prize awaiting when you successfully finish God's course: "To him who overcomes, I will grant to sit with me on my throne" (Rev. 3:21).

There's an amazing crown of life for all who run the race and persevere to the finish line with Jesus Christ. The prize is worth all the pain and struggle of running the race. Jesus will be there to joyfully greet us face to face, and we will be forever free of the struggles and bonds that hindered us in this life. Finally, we will be in such utter awe and amazement of Jesus that we will celebrate, explore, love, and worship Him for all eternity. It will be more than mere worship for a lifetime. It will be perfect, exciting, face-to-face worship of God that stretches throughout eternity.

—— **Reflections on Living a Life of Worship** ——

Our encounter with God leads to an everyday life of worship.

Perspectives

What are your first-thought perspectives and reflections on living a life of worship? What strikes you as important, interesting, or challenging?

What are some of the ways our culture of individualism works against experiencing unity in the body of Christ?

Foundations

What does "living a life of worship" personally mean to you in your everyday life? What are your challenges in doing this?

What do repentance (a new route) and worship have to do with each other?

What are some of your experiences in living a life of worship? In listening and following God's leading? In "Here I am. Send me!" experiences? In following God's path through dry periods?

Insights

Our encounter with God leads to an everyday life of worship. It is confirmed and activated as we respond to His call to do His kingdom work on earth and live each moment as an act of worship for Him. Like Isaiah, we raise our hand and passionately plead "Here I am. Send me!"

How do you recognize when God is leading you to take a new route? In following through on your beliefs? In acting in faith despite circumstances?

When and how do you give thanks? When is it easy to respond with heartfelt thanks? When is it difficult, so that responding with thanks is something only faith can provide while persevering?

Application

How do you see Part 5's "Living" insights as challenging, changing, or reinforcing your perspectives and experience? How are you being called closer to God in worship?

How might you apply this?

EPILOGUE:
LIFE-CHANGING WORSHIP

Isaiah's story teaches us about approaching God, surrendering to Him, experiencing Him, and ultimately living life in a new way.

Our response, as Isaiah's, is the essence of what it means to worship God.

In worship, we acknowledge our Mighty God with hearts of wonder and gratefulness, and we respond in a life of obedience and service.

Chapter 26

EMBERS

Campfires

I have many great memories of time spent at the lake in northwestern Minnesota. Those memories include nights spent around a campfire with family and friends. Thinking about those times, I have come to realize there is a kind of progression and momentum in the life of a campfire as it passes through these phases:

- Begins with anticipation in preparing and starting the fire
- Moves into the measured process of feeding the fire as it becomes established and starts to grow
- Transitions into a blaze that draws some people closer and drives others farther away, depending on the wind, smoke, and heat
- Settles into the relaxing time when the fire becomes a comfortable friend around which we share stories and the joy

147

of simply being together. During this time, the wood burns into glowing embers that beg you to look up at the stars above and possibly roast some marshmallows for s'mores. These are the precious, fleeting times I remember most, almost as if we glowed along with the embers, producing snapping sparks that rose into the sky like fireflies.

The afterglow of encountering God in worship has the same effect. Isaiah experienced it and let the embers of his God-encounter glow through decades of a life given to God in worship. We read in Exodus 33 that Moses's face glowed long after his glimpse of the glory of God—and that was just from seeing God's back. As we begin to encounter God in worship, we will go through a dynamic process that ebbs and flows through life:

- Being apprehensive and excited as we worship God in a new and vibrant way
- Learning and growing as the fire of worship is established in our hearts and lives
- Relating in new ways, as the flame of life-encompassing worship is activated in us, causing some people to draw closer to God and others to back away
- Coming together with like-hearted people to share God's Word, prayer, songs, and real stories of what God has done for us

The Glow of God

True worship causes us to carry the glow of God's presence within us long after an encounter with God in worship. Why? Because we are God's living embers in the world.

What does the glow of God look like? Among other expressions, it looks like the following:

- A grateful, saved people who live with a deep compassion and love for God and for other people
- Hope in the midst of fear and despair
- Love that puts other people's needs in front of our own desires—not because we're supposed to, but because we want to
- Integrity in our dealings with all people
- Service that overflows from a vigilant desire to serve
- Faith lived out in a life fully given over to God as we listen to and follow Him closely
- Fresh, new people who are doing life differently from what our world sets as the standard

The Apostle Paul said, "So here's what I want you to do, with God helping you":

Take your everyday, ordinary life—your sleeping, eating, going-to-work, and walking-around life—and place it before God as an offering. Embracing what God does for you is the best thing you can do for him. Don't become so well-adjusted to your culture that you fit into it without even thinking. Instead, fix your attention on God. You'll be changed from the inside out. Readily recognize what he wants from you, and quickly respond to it. Unlike the culture around you, always dragging you down to its level of immaturity, God brings the best out of you, develops well-formed maturity in you. (Rom. 12:1–2, MSG)

Unlike a campfire, the embers within Christ-followers don't die out, even beyond the realm of this life. The Bible describes with stunning beauty the coming reality of the time that is approaching, when all who have said yes to Jesus Christ will be with Him forever in new bodies that will never be sad or sick, and will never die:

Then the Angel showed me Water-of-Life River, crystal bright. It flowed from the Throne of God and the Lamb, right down the middle of the street. The Tree of Life was planted on each side of the River, producing twelve kinds of fruit, a ripe fruit each month. The leaves of the Tree are for healing the nations. Never again will anything be cursed. The Throne of God and of the Lamb is at the center. His servants will offer God service—worshipping, they'll look on his face, their foreheads mirroring God. Never again will there be any night. No one will need lamplight or sunlight. The shining of God, the Master, is all the light anyone needs. And they will rule with him age after age. (Rev. 22:1–5, MSG)

On that day, our worship will be fulfilled by the joy of actually, physically being in the presence of God. We will brightly reflect His glory and everlasting love as we go through eternity with Him.

Until then, let the embers of God-empowered worship glow in and through you. That's worship for a lifetime.

Chapter 27

THE HEAVENLY
THRONE ROOM REVISITED

Have you ever tried to describe something, only to find words are not enough to convey its beauty and wonder? The first time I saw the northern lights, I was almost speechless. To this day, I can't accurately describe the brilliant, dancing colors that filled the sky that night in northern Minnesota. Words don't do justice to my experience. You had to be there.

Like the Isaiah encounter, another heavenly worship event is described in the fourth and fifth chapters of the book of Revelation, the last book of the Bible. When reading this account, it's important to understand the focus and biblical symbols of this experience; otherwise, it's easy to get bogged down and confused with the unfamiliar and fantastic things taking place. Keep in mind that John was trying to describe with words something far beyond his human experience and ability to clearly express.

The focus of this encounter is God's unrivaled splendor and the glorious appearance of Jesus Christ, which causes every creature to sing and bow in worship.

John's Revelation Vision

In this account, John describes a vision that bears some resemblance to Isaiah's encounter with God. Like Isaiah, John was invited to enter into the heavenly worship experience. He approached the throne of God in amazement and awe as he witnessed the sight of God's glory. He saw God firmly in control, on the seat of ultimate power and authority. In the rainbow that surrounded God, John realized that a new covenant was now in place. This covenant was one of eternal life, like the green emerald throne on which the risen, glorified Jesus Christ now sits.

At that moment, John knew that Jesus—God in the flesh—is the everlasting King, the source of eternal Life, and the new covenant.

Jesus's brilliant appearance in heaven is described as resembling the precious gemstones jasper and sardius. Jasper is pure white and translucent, just as the resurrected Jesus is radiant and perfectly holy. Sardius is deep red in color, like the blood Jesus shed on the cross. It's also important to note that these stones are the first and last stones in the breastplate of the High Priest.

At the sight of these gemstones, John also understood that Jesus is more than the Eternal King. He's also the perfect, holy, and eternal High Priest, who is able to represent all people who know and trust Him for their salvation.

Unlike Isaiah, John saw other people engaged in this heavenly worship experience! The Revelation account calls these people the twenty-four elders. Many Scripture scholars believe they represent all believers in Jesus Christ. These people are wearing the white robes of righteousness given to them by Jesus as a sign that they were washed clean by Him. They are also wearing gold crowns, gifts from Jesus that represent both eternal life and the reward for persevering in lives of service to Him.

John heard and felt heaven moving and shaking. This time the thunder, lightning, and rumblings came directly from God's throne. God was at work, speaking and moving with power! John also noted a heavenly sea of calm, perfect peace and order that stood in front of God's throne. He witnessed the ever-burning presence of the Holy Spirit, lighting the world through the fellowship of Christ-followers, the Church.

John also saw magnificent, heavenly beings. Similar to the song of the Seraphim of Isaiah's encounter, these beings worshiped the eternal God with singing:

Holy, holy, holy is the Lord God Almighty, Who was, and is, and is to come. (Rev. 4:8)

It's easy to focus on their unique and powerful features. But that isn't the point. Like mirrors, these impressive heavenly beings appear to reflect the attributes of the risen Jesus Christ:

- One creature looked like a lion, reflecting Jesus, who is the Lion of Judah. Like a family crest, the lion is the symbol of the tribe of Judah, and the promised Messiah was foretold to come out of this lineage.
- Another creature resembled an ox; the animal that serves by carrying heavy burdens. Jesus became the suffering servant who carried the immense burden of the sins of all people who

say yes to Him. To this day, He carries the burdens of all who come to Him!

- A third heavenly being looked like a man. Jesus is fully God, who took on our humanity to pay the price for our sins and atonement.
- The last heavenly creature looked like an eagle, the symbol of swift power and authority. This heavenly being reflected the fact that Jesus is truly and fully God.

Reflecting God's Glory is the result of true worship. It's not hard to see that whenever these living creatures worship God, there is an echo and reverberation of praise that follows, beginning with the church gathered around the throne of God. It is a song of praise lifted to the Creator of all things.

The Scroll with Seven Seals

In the midst of this jubilant worship, something unsettling takes place. John sees God the Father holding an extremely important scroll with seven seals. Like Isaiah, he wept—more accurately, wailed in grief—that no one was worthy to open the scrolls.

What was the big deal with this scroll that would cause John to be so devastated when he thought no one could open it? In John's time, scrolls often served as real estate title documents or as royal decrees and wills. They were legally binding documents or decrees that had a brief summary of their detailed contents on the outside.

Could it be that this scroll is the key to the fulfillment of God's plan for the redemption of people and the entire cosmos? If this scroll is God's "real estate document," it is evidence of God's ownership of all things. John also understood that this document would reveal the events and "closing date" of the future, cosmos-changing event. If this scroll is the record of God's will, it would reveal when and how God will intervene to consummate the plan Jesus fulfilled, a plan that will ultimately bring about a new heaven and earth.

There's at least one other possibility. Scrolls were also part of the public record of John's time, an important document filed when someone defaulted on his debts or lost his land. Often people became enslaved because of their land debts until a kinsman (a relative) known as their "redeemer" would purchase or redeem the land on their behalf and allow them to be set free. The Old Testament word *Goel* was sometimes used to describe this kinsman-redeemer who would bring and buy back those enslaved in debt.

It makes sense to consider that this is why John wept so loudly. It appeared there was no man, no kinsman-redeemer, who could pay the debt of humanity's sins. Like Isaiah, John wept for the devastating eternal consequences for all people. No one could stand before God, for all were unworthy and would remain forever enslaved. No human had the position, the sinless status, the willingness, and the resources required to free people. Things looked hopeless.

Jesus, Our Glorified Redeemer

Then one of the elders, a representative of the church gathered in heaven, approached John with extremely Good News: there *is* someone who can take the scroll and open the seals. This man is the promised Messiah (the Lion of Judah) from the royal line of Jesse (the Root of David). He is worthy, able, and willing to be the kinsman-redeemer that all people desperately need.

Then John saw a spotless Lamb that appeared to be slain.

John knew this was Jesus Christ, the spotless, sinless man who took upon Himself the sin-debts of people and became the pure sacrifice and payment for their redemption. The Lamb is Jesus. He is our kinsman, a human being. He lived a perfect, sin-free life. He willingly paid the price for our redemption on the cross with His blood and life. Jesus, the Son of God, perfectly and completely accomplished the required sacrifice for our salvation. Encircled with the praise of the living creatures and the church, Jesus Christ humbly and freely takes the scroll from the right hand of God. He alone is worthy and able to do this.

And the deal is done. Enslaved, hopeless people are set free. The Creator and holder of the cosmos paid the price Himself. The momentum of events that will lead to the ultimate, victorious inauguration of a new heaven, new earth, and new reality free of sin, sickness, death, and evil is underway. God's will for all creation is unsealed and in motion.

Then an amazing thing takes place. All in heaven, beginning with the church and extending to all the angels and heavenly beings, encircle the Lamb of God in songs of worship. Soon all living creatures are joining in worshipping God and the victorious Lamb, Jesus Christ.

It's all about Jesus. He's the King, the High Priest, the Lion, the Suffering Servant, the Man, the Swift Ruler, the Kinsman-Redeemer, the Lamb of God, and so much more.

Worship for an Eternity

At its heart, worship is the ongoing, eternal experience of all who have been redeemed by Jesus Christ. When we know Him and are living in the new reality of His presence within us, we'll join with all heaven in encircling God with praise and thanks, our very life proclaiming what they sing:

To him who sits on the throne and to the Lamb be praise and honor and glory and power, for ever and ever! (Rev. 5:13)

Chapter 28
WORSHIP COMMITMENT PRAYER

Lord God,

You are infinitely worthy of the praises of all heaven and the cosmos. I commit myself to worship you alone.

I am amazed by who you are and all you have done for me. My response is to accept and respond to your love in worship.

I commit to do the following:

- *Approach you* in worship with awe, humility, and gratefulness. I cast aside my selfish agendas and preferences and come ready to give you the authentic offering of praise you deserve.
- *Surrender to you* in worship, allowing you to transform and mold me into the person you desire me to be. Reveal the areas of my life that need to be cleansed, and renew me so I will worship you free of all impediments.

- *Accept your invitation* to taste, see, hear, and experience you in worship. Meeting with you, my Lord and God, is the goal of my worship. I will no longer keep you at arm's length, but will seek to know you even more.
- *Serve you*, with your power and Word living in me. I will activate and extend my worship to the people, moments, and the circumstances of my life. I know you will use a life fully given in worship to draw more people to you.

Lord, I offer my worship and my love, not just for a moment, time, or place, but for all my lifetime and into eternity.

In Jesus's name I pray. Amen.

Reflections on Life-Changing Worship

Isaiah's story teaches us about approaching God, surrendering to Him, experiencing Him, and ultimately living life in a new way.

Perspectives

What are your wrap-up perspectives and reflections on Isaiah's life-changing encounter with God?

What themes strike you as important to embed in your life?

Foundations

As a result of this study, how have your perspectives on worship and living a life of worship changed?

Insights

Isaiah's story teaches us about approaching God, surrendering to Him, experiencing Him, and ultimately living life in a new way. Our response, as Isaiah's, is the essence of what it means to worship God.

What new insights have you gained regarding Approaching, Surrendering, Experiencing, and Living a life of everyday worship?

What thoughts do you have on the "glow of God's presence" being reflected in everyday worship?

What reflections do you have regarding John's Revelation vision of the unrivaled splendor and the glorious appearance of Jesus Christ?

What "next steps" is God calling you to take in reflecting the glow of His grace?

Application

Pray the Worship Commitment Prayer.

Live an everyday life of worship!

ISAIAH CHAPTER 6 (NASB)

Isaiah's Vision

[1] In the year of King Uzziah's death I saw the Lord sitting on a throne, lofty and exalted, with the train of His robe filling the temple. [2] Seraphim stood above Him, each having six wings: with two he covered his face, and with two he covered his feet, and with two he flew. [3] And one called out to another and said,

> "Holy, Holy, Holy, is the LORD of hosts,
> The whole earth is full of His glory."

[4] And the foundations of the thresholds trembled at the voice of him who called out, while the temple was filling with smoke. [5] Then I said,
> "Woe is me, for I am ruined!
> Because I am a man of unclean lips,
> And I live among a people of unclean lips;

For my eyes have seen the King, the Lord of hosts."

[6] Then one of the seraphim flew to me with a burning coal in his hand, which he had taken from the altar with tongs. [7] He touched my mouth *with it* and said, "Behold, this has touched your lips; and your iniquity is taken away and your sin is forgiven."

Isaiah's Commission

[8] Then I heard the voice of the Lord, saying, "Whom shall I send, and who will go for Us?" Then I said, "Here am I. Send me!" [9] He said, "Go, and tell this people:

> 'Keep on listening, but do not perceive;
> Keep on looking, but do not understand.
> [10] "Render the hearts of this people insensitive,
> Their ears dull,
> And their eyes dim,
> Otherwise they might see with their eyes,
> Hear with their ears,
> Understand with their hearts,
> And return and be healed."

[11] Then I said, "Lord, how long?" And He answered,

> "Until cities are devastated and without inhabitant,
> Houses are without people
> And the land is utterly desolate,
> [12] "The Lord has removed men far away,
> And the forsaken places are many in the midst of the land.
> [13] "Yet there will be a tenth portion in it,
> And it will again be subject to burning,
> Like a terebinth or an oak
> Whose stump remains when it is felled.
> The holy seed is its stump."

A LIFE-CHANGING ENCOUNTER

Lessons for Life-Changing Worship

Isaiah was a prophet who lived more than 2,600 years ago. A defining point in Isaiah's ministry was a life-changing, face-to-face encounter with God, as described in the sixth chapter of the book of Isaiah. This momentous event in Isaiah's life provides insights about authentic, God-directed worship.

God is asking you and me to enter into the same worship experience that Isaiah knew: approaching God in worship, surrendering ourselves, experiencing God, and activating a living worship of God—not just for a moment, but in living an everyday life of worship.

In worship we acknowledge our Mighty God with hearts of wonder and gratefulness, and we respond in a life of love, obedience, and service.

Approaching God in Worship

God is the initiator of the worship process. He invites us to approach Him in worship, regardless of our social status, past accomplishments or failures, our strengths or faults. Ultimately, God desires a heart-to-heart encounter that is real and meaningful.

God calls us to a heart-to-heart encounter.

As we enter into worship, we see God's glory evidenced in who He is, what He has created, and in others who are experiencing Him firsthand.

As we approach God in worship, we come with no other agenda but awe, amazement, and gratefulness.

Surrendering Ourselves to God in Worship

God asks us to willingly and continually surrender ourselves to Him and His forgiveness, cleansing power, and grace.

As we open ourselves to God, we realize His awesome power and His deep love for us.

He wants to touch us, change us, and bring us to a better place through worship.

Even as we yield to God, we recognize that healing and grace come only from God's hand, not our efforts.

Experiencing God in Worship

The essence of worship is to experience God and be changed by His power so that we can live more and more for Him.

The essence of worship is to experience God and be changed.

This occurs both in our personal time with God and when we gather with others in God-directed and empowered worship.

When we experience God, we are filled with the energy and desire to live more and more for Him.

Living an Everyday Life of Worship

Our worship encounter with God is confirmed and activated as we respond to His call to do His kingdom work on earth and live each day and moment as an act of worship for Him.

Our encounter with God leads to an everyday life of worship.

It is confirmed and activated as we respond to His call to do His kingdom work on earth and live each day and moment as an act of worship for Him.

Like Isaiah, we raise our hand and passionately plead, "Here I am. Send me!"

STUDY GUIDE

Overview

This is a seven-week study on worship, introducing and reflecting on the foundational lessons we can learn from Isaiah about living an everyday life of worship.

The book is structured in six themed sections. Each section is composed of five chapters that present a related facet of worship. These chapters are designed as daily readings.

Reflection questions follow each section. These provide a brief reminder of the major theme and invite reflection on Going-In Perspectives, Foundational Beliefs, Gained Insights, and Personal Application.

Chris's video introductions are available on his Vimeo channel: https://vimeo.com/channels/theisaiahencounter, or by going to www.chrisatkins.net. Follow Chris and his blog at www.chrisatkins.net for these and other resources.

Week 1: Introduction & Kickoff

Introduction:
- Together (rotationally), read the "Preface: Perspectives" page.
- Kick off the study by exploring going-in definitions and thoughts on worship.
- Consider why God created worship.
- Invite sharing as to where and how worship is experienced.

Group Study:
- Together (rotationally) read Isaiah chapter 6, which tells the story of Isaiah's life-changing experience with God.
- Share reflections and insights on this reading.

Assignment:
- During the week, read *The Isaiah Encounter,* chapters 1–5. Prepare answers to the reflection questions.

Week 2: Worship (Isaiah 6)

Video:
- View Chris's video introduction to *The Isaiah Encounter* on his Vimeo channel at https://vimeo.com/channels/theisaiahencounter, or by going to www.chrisatkins.net.

Group Study:
- Again read Isaiah chapter 6 together.
- Referencing Isaiah 6 and *The Isaiah Encounter,* chapters 1–5, what ideas or insights come to your attention?
- Review the section theme and definition of worship.
- How do you relate to this?
- Invite discussion based on each of the reflection questions.

Assignment:

- During the week, read *The Isaiah Encounter,* chapters 6–10. Prepare answers to the reflection questions.

Week 3: Approaching God in Worship

Video:

- View Chris's video introduction to "Approaching God in Worship" on his Vimeo channel at https://vimeo.com/channels/theisaiahencounter, or by going to www.chrisatkins.net.

Group Study:

- Review the section theme: God calls us to a heart-to-heart encounter.
- How do you relate to this?
- Review the themes for chapters 6–10. What ideas or insights come to your attention?
- Invite discussion based on each of the reflection questions.

Assignment:

- During the week, read *The Isaiah Encounter,* chapters 11–15. Prepare answers to the reflection questions.

Week 4: Surrendering to God in Worship

Video:

- View Chris's video introduction to "Surrendering to God in Worship" on his Vimeo channel at https://vimeo.com/channels/theisaiahencounter, or by going to www.chrisatkins.net.

Group Study:

- Review the section theme: as we open ourselves to God, we realize He loves us deeply.
- How do you relate to this?

- Review the themes for chapters 11–15. What ideas or insights come to your attention?
- Invite discussion based on each of the reflection questions.

Assignment:
- During the week, read *The Isaiah Encounter,* chapters 16–20. Prepare answers to the reflection questions.

Week 5: Experiencing God in Worship

Video:
- View Chris's video introduction to "Experiencing God in Worship" on his Vimeo channel at https://vimeo.com/channels/theisaiahencounter, or by going to www.chrisatkins.net.

Group Study:
- Review the section theme: God calls us to a heart-to-heart encounter.
- How do you relate to this?
- Review the themes for chapters 16–20. What ideas or insights come to your attention?
- Invite discussion based on each of the reflection questions.

Assignment:
- During the week, read *The Isaiah Encounter,* chapters 21–25. Prepare answers to the reflection questions.

Week 6: Living a Life of Worship

Video:
- View Chris's video introduction to "Living a Life of Worship" on his Vimeo channel at https://vimeo.com/channels/theisaiahencounter, or by going to www.chrisatkins.net.

Group Study:
- Review the section theme: the essence of worship is to experience God and be changed.
- How do you relate to this?
- Review the themes for chapters 21–25. What ideas or insights come to your attention?
- Invite discussion based on each of the reflection questions.

Assignment:
- During the week, read *The Isaiah Encounter,* chapters 26–27. Reread Isaiah chapter 6. Prepare answers to the reflection questions.

Week 7: Life-Changing Worship

Group Study:
- Review *The Isaiah Encounter,* chapters 26–27. What ideas or insights come to your attention?
- Invite discussion based on each of the reflection questions.
- Together (rotationally) read the Worship Commitment Prayer (chapter 28).

Assignment:
- Live an everyday life of worship!

We invite your feedback!

We invite and appreciate your comments, suggestions, and stories!

Contact Chris at chris.atkins.author@gmail.com.

Follow Chris and join his blog at www.ChrisAtkins.net.

WORKS CITED

William Booth, "A Merry Christmas: Is Any Merry, Let Him Sing,"
The War Cry: Official Gazette of the Salvation Army, No.53
(London, December, 1880), 1.

Kirk Dearman, "We Bring the Sacrifice of Praise" (Brentwood-Benson
Music Publishing, Inc., 1984)

Charlotte Elliot, "Just As I Am," The Christian Remembrancer (1835)

Charles Finney, Lectures on Revival (Bloomington, MN: Bethany
House, 1989)

William Temple, Readings in St. John's Gospel: Compiled from the
Gifford Lectures given in Glasgow between November 1932 and
March 1934 by William Temple (London, MacMillan and Co,
LTD, 1945)

Benjamin D. Williams, "Early Christian Liturgics: Early Christian
Worship Had Its Origins in Jewish Forms and Practices"
(Liturgica.com, http://www.liturgica.com/html/litEChLit.jsp)

ACKNOWLEDGMENTS

I thank God for the people who have supported and walked this journey with me, especially my family:

My beautiful wife, Terese

My amazing children: Nate, Greg, Alyssa, and Annie

My daughters-in-law: Brenda and Lindsey

My precious grandchildren: Ruby, Juneau, and Wynden

There are four people whose inspiration, support, and tireless work have helped make this book a reality. Tom, Terri, Jann, and Mike, thank you for your dedication to God and His kingdom work. It is my privilege to serve alongside you.

ABOUT THE AUTHOR

Chris Atkins is a worship leader, pastor, ministry consultant, and songwriter with a passion for helping individuals experience God's indwelling presence in their lives. He is the founder of Grace Unleashed, Inc., a Christian outreach ministry focused on inviting individuals to know Jesus Christ, equipping believers in their walk, and worshipping together.

Chris holds a B.A. in Christian Ministry from Bethel University and has served as an adjunct professor, teaching worship to seminary students. He has helped churches develop vibrant worship ministries and is recognized as a mentor and encourager of young worship leaders.

With thirty years of experience in serving God and His church, Chris shares spiritual, ministerial, and practical lessons in worship conferences, speaking engagements, videos, and written works.

Chris and his wife Terese make their home in Minneapolis, Minnesota.

Contact Chris at chris.atkins.author@gmail.com.

Follow Chris and join in his blog at www.ChrisAtkins.net.

Printed in the USA
CPSIA information can be obtained
at www.ICGtesting.com
JSHW022343140824
68134JS00019B/1656